"IN TELLING HIS POWERFUL STORY, ROBERT King keeps the light shining on the struggle for human rights and justice."
HARRY BELAFONTE

"MARTIN LUTHER KING REMINDED US THAT 'our lives begin to end the day we become silent about things that matter.' Robert King is very much alive and still fighting for justice. This book is a must-read!"
COLIN AND LIVIA FIRTH

"LESS THAN TWO MONTHS FROM HIS 70TH year of sojourn on the planet, and the 40th anniversary of A3's stint in solitary confinement, Robert Hillary King goes back to the bottom of the heap to extract quicksilver and lines of turquoise. This new edition contains a collection of essays on volatile topics like the n word and executed POWs Shaka Sankofa a.k.a. Gary Graham (June 2000) and Troy Anthony Davis (September 2011). The book is also an annotated look at one man's quest to alert the world about the conditions inside a system that punishes those who think differently. As relevant now as it was in 2009, perhaps even more so, From the Bottom of the Heap: The Autobiography of Black Panther Robert Hillary King, shows how despite the residual psychological effects of captivity — solitary confinement at that — one's humanity can be saved. This little book, by a brave and thoughtful man, can serve as a blueprint for those on the front line both in minimum and maximum security America."
WANDA SABIR Cofounder and CEO of Maafa San Francisco Bay Area; WandasPicks.com

"KING'S WORDS PERCOLATE WITH THE urgency and determination that made the Panthers once one of North America's most revolutionary units.... Though Louisiana has yet to atone for the wasted years given by the trio of Black Panther organizers, *From the Bottom of the Heap* is one man's shot at making sure a history and a struggle are not lost now or to future generations."
ERNESTO AGUILAR *Political Media Review*

"THE CIRCUMSTANCES AND TRUE-TO-LIFE stories described in *From the Bottom of the Heap* illustrate that there

are multiple and diverse African-American experiences in the U.S., experiences that range from the White House to prison walls."
STEFAN CHRISTOFF *The Hour*

"WHEN ROBERT KING WAS RELEASED FROM Angola, he declared, 'Even though I was free from Angola, Angola would never be free of me.' With this book, King makes good on his promise."
MEL MOTEL *WIN* magazine

"ALBERT WOODFOX, HERMAN WALLACE AND Robert Wilkerson are worth my efforts and the efforts of all who believe that you must fight injustice where you find it."
DAME ANITA RODDICK Cofounder of The Body Shop and human rights activist

"THE RELENTLESS PROSECUTION OF THE Angola 3 in the infamous Penitentiary at Angola . . . is another in a long line of cases in this country involving egregious prosecutorial misconduct. The interests of justice can only be served by ending the prosecution and dropping the charges against them, and setting them free."
RAMSEY CLARK Former U.S. Attorney General

"FRIENDSHIPS ARE FORGED IN STRANGE places. My friendship with Robert King, and the other two Angola 3 men Herman Wallace and Albert Woodfox, is based on respect. These men, as Robert reveals in this stunning account of his life, have fought tirelessly to redress injustice, not only for themselves, but for others. Since his release in 2001 Robert has been engaged in the fight to rescue these men from a cruel and repressive administration that colludes in deliberate lying and obfuscation to keep them locked up. This is a battle Robert is determined to win, and we are determined to help him."
GORDON RODDICK Cofounder of The Body Shop and human rights activist

"THIS BOOK IS A SEARING INDICTMENT OF THE contemporary USA, a rich and commanding nation, which still crushes the hopes and aspirations of so many poor Black Americans and criminalizes their young. Robert Hillary King's account of his horrifying 29 years in prison for a crime he did not commit should shame all of us who believe that justice has to be at the heart of any democracy worthy of that name."

(BARONESS) HELENA KENNEDY QC Member of the House of Lords, Chair of Justice, UK

"WHEN THERE IS A TRAIN WRECK, THERE IS A public inquiry, to try to avoid it recurring. Robert King's conviction was a train wreck, and this book is perhaps the only way the world will get to understand why. There are more than 3,000 people serving life without the possibility of parole in Angola today, some as young as 14 when they were sent there, and many of them innocent but without the lawyer to prove it. We owe it to them, and others in a similar plight around the world, to read this book. And Robert King wears a mighty fine hat!"

CLIVE STAFFORD SMITH Director, Reprieve

"AS A BRUSH WITH DEATH SHARPENS LIFE, A lifetime of confinement can broaden the vision . . . "

AUSTIN AMERICAN STATESMAN

". . . DISTURBED BY EVIDENCE SUGGESTING that their long term isolation may have been based, at least in part, on their past activism and association with the Black Panther Party . . . the prisoners' prolonged isolation breached international treaties which the USA has ratified . . . The relevant treaties have found that prolonged solitary confinement can amount to torture or cruel, inhuman or degrading treatment."

AMNESTY INTERNATIONAL on the Angola 3, 2007

"THEIR ADHERENCE TO THE BLACK Panther ideology has given them the strength, courage and spirit to fight the prison system."

DAVID HILLIARD Former Black Panther Party Chief of Staff

" . . . THERE IS POWERFUL EVIDENCE THAT they were framed . . . despite the compelling evidence of a terrible miscarriage of justice, Woodfox and Wallace remain locked up . . ."

INDEPENDENT TELEVISION NEWS UK

"THEY ENDURED AND SURVIVED OVER ALL these years with very little help from the outside. They are the kind of unsung heroes who we must come forward to help because they never asked for anything from us in exchange for what they have suffered."
GERONIMO JI JAGA Former Minister of Defense Black Panther Party and former U.S. political prisoner

"FACED WITH LIFE WITHOUT PAROLE IN SOLI-tary, it is past time for us to organize for their lives to be lived in freedom. They are political prisoners of the highest caliber who deserve your support."
MUMIA ABU-JAMAL Former Black Panther, and U.S. Political Prisoner on Death Row

"THESE KINDS OF WARRIORS MUST NEVER BE forgotten. They have been at the front line of the struggle, fighting against the worst kind of brutalities and humiliations."
YURI KOCHIYAMA Human Rights Activist

"I RECENTLY BECAME AWARE OF EVIDENCE that suggests these men were wrongly convicted. I urge a swift and just resolution of the matter."
JOHN CONYERS U.S. Ranking Congressmen and Chairman of the U.S. House Judiciary Committee

"WE KNOW FROM GUANTÁNAMO BAY AND other notorious prisons that keeping detainees in solitary confinement for extended periods of time can be extremely damaging and it is truly shocking that the Louisiana state authorities saw fit to inflict decades of solitary on 'the Angola 3.' Robert King's book is a timely expose of past injustice as well as a call to action. It deserves to be read by anyone with even a passing interest in the United States, justice and human rights."
KATE ALLEN Amnesty International UK director

"TO LOSE ONES FREEDOM IS A TERRIBLE punishment in itself. To be innocent and incarcerated for 29 years is almost beyond belief. Robert King survived this experience with his dignity intact and with a renewed passion for justice. An amazing story."
TERRY WAITE CBE

FROM THE BOTTOM OF THE HEAP

PM PRESS

FROM THE BOTTOM OF THE HEAP

THE AUTOBIOGRAPHY OF BLACK PANTHER ROBERT HILLARY KING

FROM THE BOTTOM OF THE HEAP:
THE AUTOBIOGRAPHY OF BLACK PANTHER ROBERT HILLARY KING
BY ROBERT HILLARY KING

Published by:
PM Press
PO Box 23912
Oakland, CA 94623
www.pmpress.org

Cover photograph by Ann Harkness
Angola 3 illustration by Rigo 23
Robert King illustration by Emory Douglas

ISBN: 978-1-60486-575-2
Library Of Congress Control Number: 2012945337

10 9 8 7 6 5 4 3 2

Printed in the USA on recycled paper,
by the Employee Owners of Thomson-Shore in Dexter, Michigan.
www.thomsonshore.com

DEDICATED TO

The memory of Anita Roddick: activist, humanitarian, benefactor, and friend; 1942–2007.

CONTENTS

ACKNOWLEDGEMENTS

REVOLUTIONARY LOVE AND REGARDS TO

Herman Wallace and Albert Woodfox, who have kept the commitment to truth throughout these years and have continued to pay for it by being held in solitary for over thirty-six years. Your freedom is inevitable.

Special thanks to Rigo 23, a friend and ardent supporter of the Angola 3, Mumia Abu-Jamal, Leonard Peltier, and other political prisoners for many years. Rigo chooses anonymity, but his artwork and activism denies his wishes to remain anonymous.

Special thanks to scott crow, Cofounder of Common Ground Collective, and many other visionary grassroots projects. His urgent persistence, hard work, and enthusiasm was the inspiration I needed in a time of crisis to continue this work.

I would like to thank my two cousins Doris and Audrey for their genealogical research into family history. Their contribution is highly appreciated.

A whole chapter could be written just about Marina Drummer and her efforts to highlight the case of the Angola 3. Besides giving herself wholeheartedly to see us collectively achieve releases from prison, she inspired me individually with her own assessment of our case, likening it to that of Mumia Abu-Jamal, saying, "Just as Mumia is poster child for those wrongfully incarcerated on death row, Angola 3 are the poster children for those wrongfully incarcerated in prison." It was this analysis and assessment that inspired me more than a decade ago, and this likening has continued to inspire me to this day. Thanks, Marina.

I would also like to thank Mark Child and Joanna Tamburino for their efforts on behalf of the Angola 3 and for their research.

I would like to thank Nina Kowalska for her discipline, in-depth knowledge, expertise, and skills she has contributed to the campaign. She was an invaluable asset. Without her, this, the second coming of this book could not have happened.

My deepest gratitude and recognition to:

Ann Harkness, my sister in struggle, for working behind the scenes on my candy business and for all the things you do. You're a warrior.

NPR's Kitchen Sisters, Davia Nelson and Nikki Silva, for keeping my candy business and the story of the A3 alive.

Gordon Roddick and Samantha Roddick, for keeping alive the legacy of your wife and mother Anita Roddick.

Marion Brown, cofounder of A3 Support Committee, my longtime comrade, for not forgetting.

Malik Rahim, cofounder of A3 Support Committee and Common Ground Collective, for not giving up the fight for justice all these years in New Orleans.

Gail Shaw and Billy X, cofounders of the A3 Support Committee and It's about Time, and Althea Francois, cofounder of A3 Support Committee.

Cola Robbins Owens, a teacher at Tougaloo College, Mississippi who showed me some of the ways of writing.

My heartfelt appreciation and thanks to many longtime friends and comrades who shared so much and have never given up. Bruce Allen, Orissa Arend, Brackin "Firecracker" Camp, Col. Nyati Bolt, Scott Fleming, James Clark, Shana Griffin, Anne Pruden, Jackie Sumell, Brice White, Chris Aberley, Millie Barnet, Brooke Biggs, Linda Carmichael, Tristesse Casimer, Geronimo Ji Jaga and the Kuji Foundation, Mumia Abu-Jamal, Anja DeGraff, Leslie George, Noelle Hanrahan and Prison Radio, Pam Holbrook, Erin Howley, Elizabeth Jeffers, Mwalimu Johnson, M.T. Karthik, Anake Konig, Mark and Anna Chiat, Anna Kraakman, Laurie Lazer, Cesar Maxit, Billie Mizell, Sarah Myers, Carrie Reichardt, Wanda Sabir (of Wanda's Picks), Kalil Shayid, Dave Strano, Tajiri (Truth Universal), Luis "Bato" Talamantez and California Prison Focus, Ron Chisom and The Peoples Institute for Survival and Beyond, Akeilah, Khadijah and Jamilla, of the Community Defender, Garilla Ballard, Violetta Thompson (now an ancestor), Anita Yesho, Yasmine, and Raul Salinas (now an ancestor). Thanks to all of our supporters overseas in the UK, Portugal, Belgium, and many other countries I have visited during my travels.

Special thanks to Chuck and all on our "A3 Team" for your work behind the scenes.

Thanks to David Martinez, for your presence to welcome me as I first walked free.

Thanks to PM Press: Ramsey Kanaan, Terry Bisson for the original editing of the words, and to everyone working behind the scenes at PM to bring this to life. And what can I say about my editor, Ms Andrea Gibbons, except that she epitomizes the essence of editorializing as she has shown in this writing. I have words to declare her skills, but words cannot declare her dedication to this book.

My indebtedness to all the readers and advisers of this book who gave feedback over the years, thank you for your input, patience and work to see it through. It has been a long time coming.

Thanks to the people who transcribed my original manuscript, typed on an old manual typewriter that was largely written while I was in solitary at Angola Prison: Charlene Rose, Clancy Rose, Evan St. John, Austin Van Zant, James Clark, Erin Howley, and scott crow.

Revolutionary love to all former members of the Black Panther Party for putting their lives on the line for the ideals, dedication and commitment to bring about revolutionary change in this country. The legacy lives on.

And lastly thanks and deepest recognition to all the longtime and recent empathizers, sympathizers around the world and who have given their time and dedication to free Herman Wallace, Albert Woodfox, myself and all political prisoners over the years. Thank you for helping to bring these injustices to the forefront.

If I omitted anyone it was an honest mistake, my apologies and sincere thanks for everything you have done too!!

Free the Angola 3!
Free ALL political prisoners and prisoners of conscience!
All Power to the People!

ROBERT KING
a.k.a. Robert King Wilkerson 2008

RUMINATIONS ON FROM THE BOTTOM... MUMIA ABU-JAMAL, M.A.

WHAT, ONE WONDERS, IS IN A NAME?

A curse? A blessing? A mystery?

For Robert Hillary King (the man formerly known as Robert King Wilkerson) that question must be a haunting one. For he spent over 50 years — a lifetime — with a name not his own; only learning his "true" name after escaping the clutches of one of the most nefarious, violent, and deadly places on earth: the prison (formerly known as a slave plantation) called Angola.

But for Robert, his life was full of false names, ones hurled at him from courts of law like hot venom from cobras: convict, murderer, guilty, robber, *nigger.*

Like the name he bore and the name that filled his legal filings and voluminous court documents, and the cards which festooned a name and prison number in the front of dozens of cells in numerous hells which his *proud* flesh occupied for three decades. *It was not him.*

Framed, damned, beaten, bludgeoned, tortured, and condemned to a living death in solitary confinement *for almost 30 years.* Robert Hillary King saw the true face of American terrorism — up close. In the contorted faces of Louisiana prison guards, and their minions, cruel "deputies" (so-called "trustees" — prisoners working for the joint), venal judges and prosecutors, they saw hell in its truest forms.

King and his comrades, Albert Woodfox and Herman Wallace, saw something else as well: that innocence was irrelevant.

The 3 men, who came to be known as the Angola 3, riled the britches of their keepers when they committed the impermissible sin of resistance to repression, by having the audacity to form a chapter of the Black Panther Party — *in prison*!

The Black Panther Party wasn't the NAACP. For this — for this violation to the White Empire, these 3 Black men had to pay — and, as of this writing, whilst Robert may be free (or as "free" as a Black man can be in America), two of the 3 — Herman and Albert — have spent 40 years — *40 years!* — in solitary confinement — solely for their political beliefs and associations.

Forty years.

Four decades of imprisonment in a stinking, rat-infested sewer about the size of a tollbooth. In Louisiana. In Angola and its environs.

In modern-day slave plantations.

The greatest violation a slave could make was resistance — and these 3 men did it, and have paid the price ever since.

In the introduction written by the esteemed Dr. Terry A. Kupers, he quotes testimony from Angola's then-Warden, Burl Cain, for the proposition that the Angola 3 weren't "good men," for they still held "their political beliefs." Amazingly, the same was said about the late, great Deputy Minister of Defense for the Los Angeles chapter of the Black Panther Party, Geronimo Ji Jaga (né Pratt). When he filed his writ, the city opposed him, saying, "He's still a revolutionary!"

And that was his and their only crime.

What kind of "good men" lock up innocent men, and torture them — for decades? What kind of system? What kind of country?

This kind. The American Empire. "*The Bottom...*"

Robert Hillary King writes from that America into which he was born, grew, and blistered under the searing heat of white hatred. It was in that hell that he existed for nearly three decades, and into that same world that he was delivered when he won his "freedom."

But, like Harriet Tubman, he ain't free until Herman Wallace and Albert Woodfox are free. He ain't free until his People are free.

And how free are we?

Law professor Michelle Alexander, in her recently published *The New Jim Crow*, argues that there are more Black men in prison cages in America then under the apartheid regime in South Africa — at its height! That more Black men are in prisons and cells than at the eve of the Civil War — when millions were in slavery!

Alexander's response to this horrendous state of affairs is to go beyond writing books — even ones like hers or Robert's. It's about building movements — *mass movements* — that act to change society. Nothing else has the slightest potential to address this unconscionable crisis.

Robert, Albert and Herman were part of just such a movement in their youth, and while it changed the nation it did not go far enough.

Some will argue that their membership in the BPP led to the horrors of their framing, incarceration, and continued isolation in solitary. And there is truth to that observation. But, were they wrong to resist against great injustice — or was that great injustice wrong? Moreover, it was precisely that Movement that gave Robert, Herman and Albert focus, insight, determination and hope. Hope, not in the system — no. But in the People, who fought for them as if for themselves

Hope. A little word, yes. But not a small thing.

The Movement educated the Angola 3, and answered the questions plaguing not only them but generations of Black end oppressed people.

Are we citizens — or subjects?

When Robert Hillary King writes of his people, his fellow denizens of Algiers, he uses the term, "colonial subject."

As a former member of the Black Panther Party, I recognize the term intuitively, as one used by the late BPP leaders, Dr. Huey P. Newton and Eldridge Cleaver.

For an empire doesn't have "citizens" — it has colonies. It has subjects. When it comes to the Black caste that peoples the U.S., it constitutes "colonial subjects": people subject to the whims of the Empire.

You have what rights that your Lords wish to grant you — and no more.

You are free — in name only, and such freedom may be snatched away at a whim, with the silent acquiescence of every court in the realm, with utter impunity.

Subjects. Unfree.

For that reason — if for no other — to quote Robert, the Struggle continues!

Until we All are free.

Mumia Abu-Jamal
Imprisoned Nation, USA

INTRODUCTION

TO ME, ROBERT HILLARY KING IS A HERO. He survived over thirty years in prison, most of them in a solitary segregation cell. After his exoneration in 2001 he emerged from prison a vital, socially conscious, and very caring leader. It could have been different. He could have emerged a bitter man, his every thought colored by a need to seek revenge for the horrible and horribly unfair years of incarceration. Or he could have shrunk from the social arena, becoming quiet and isolative like many who emerge from prison after years inside. Instead, Robert Hillary King came out of prison with a political vision, the vision that had kept him going during those years in solitary. But it's not just his political consciousness that makes him a hero; it is how he has put this consciousness into practice as he vigorously champions the cause of Herman Wallace and Albert Woodfox, the members of the Angola 3 who remain behind bars. It is how he continues to campaign passionately for the rights of all prisoners.

During Robert Hillary King's lifetime we have witnessed a drastic and tragic shift in the very purpose of the state. Under capitalism, the state has always served the interests of the rich and powerful, and always will. But traditionally there has been a split between the section of the power elite who would use the state exclusively to increase their riches, and another section of that same elite who endorse public services and social welfare programs. This liberal wing also wants to expand corporate profits. But they believe that by providing decent education, housing, and medical care to everyone, the state indirectly benefits the corporations (by fostering a more competent, healthy, and reliable workforce for example).

Roosevelt during the New Deal, and Kennedy and Johnson after him viewed the state as a provider-of-last-resort for the most disadvantaged in society. Programs included Head Start and Medicare, community mental health, low-income housing and aid to families with dependent children. It seemed by the mid-1960s as if the state was resuming its responsibility to try and provide for the most disadvantaged among us. But by the mid-1970s, as the post-WWII economic boom evaporated, the social programs were de-funded and dwindled to almost nothing. The state began to shift its focus more singularly to the maintenance of law and order and the expansion of corporate markets and profits, even when that meant waging wars. The Reagan years put the retreat from social responsibility into overdrive, as budgets for education and social welfare programs were slashed. The slashing continues today, even accelerates as wars draw heavily on the state's fiscal resources and the gap between rich and poor widens.

As the focus of the state shifted, a contradiction emerged in the public's perception. People had grown used to thinking of government as the provider of public service programs. As the government shrank its public service role, an unavoidable contradiction emerged between the notion that we live in a just society where the state helps people in great need, and the ugly reality of an ever-increasing gap between rich and poor and a worsening of the plight of those at the bottom. If we are a just and democratic society, how can we ignore children who are failed by public education? How can we and our government stand by while millions of people lose their homes? How can we tolerate the denial of health and mental health care for a growing proportion of our population?

The Prison Industrial Complex grew up in the same decades the state was busy reneging on its social responsibility. There was an urgent need to disappear the people who were harmed by the state's callousness, an urgent need to hide the contradiction created by a "democratic" society ignoring the needs of so many people. New laws make it illegal to sleep in the park or panhandle near an ATM machine, allowing the mass arrest of the homeless, and diverting attention from the fact that the wealthiest country in the world fails to insure housing for its people. A very large number of individuals suffering from mental illness have been arrested and locked up, their disappearance from the community hiding the fact that our society has reneged on its responsibility to provide adequate public mental health services. The War on Drugs has incarcerated many more, hiding the failure of inner-city schools to educate our children and the lack of living wage jobs.

The number of prisoners has expanded by leaps and bounds, past a million, past two million . . . it now approaches two and a half million people. Meanwhile, the measures taken within the prisons to control the disappeared masses and keep their stories from public view have become increasingly Draconian. They include massive overcrowding, the dismantling of rehabilitation and job training programs, long stints in segregation or the "hole," harsh restrictions on visits with families, gag orders precluding prisoners talking to the press, and the emergence of supermaximum security prisons where everyone is kept in segregation and put under the total control of officers.

I have toured many American prisons as a psychiatric expert witness in class action lawsuits over unacceptably harsh prison conditions and the sexual misconduct of male staff with women prisoners. I witness the harsh conditions, and I cite the research literature about the psychiatric damage they cause. I confess that I know a lot less about the real-time effects of prison conditions than do the men and women who are forced to live under such toxic conditions for long periods of time. Still, I am absolutely certain after interviewing over a thousand prisoners confined in segregation settings and reviewing the extant research literature, that long-term confinement in a cell where one is isolated and idle almost twenty-four hours per day causes severe pain, suffering, and psychiatric damage. In far too many cases the despair bred of long-term isolation leads to suicide.

There is a falsehood at the heart of the rationale for the imprisonment binge. The lie is the notion that, by locking up the people who would otherwise clearly remind us of the failures of our society in regard to our social responsibility, we become safer and happier. In spite of nearly two and a half million Americans incarcerated today, people are feeling both more strapped financially, and less safe in their communities than they did before the prison explosion in the 1970s and '80s. In "locking 'em up and throwing away the key," we have also broken up the families of the tens of millions of people who have been forced to spend time in jail or prison. And the average citizen has had to shut down their critical mind, and continually deny the contradiction between the USA's claim of democracy and the reality of this country disappearing so many people behind bars. The only people happy with the massive Prison Industrial Complex that has evolved over the last three decades are those who make profits or enhance their power by regimenting those condemned to incarceration.

There are among us powerful voices of protest, individuals who see clearly the contradictions between the ideals of democracy and the lies behind the Prison Industrial Complex, and who successfully get the word out about it. Robert Hillary King is such a voice. And we know what happens to the people who vociferously and effectively expose the contradictions of a callous democracy and protest the disappearing of people behind bars. History has shown us that they are targeted as dangerous dissenters, branded as criminals, arrested en masse, and sent away to prison. I have known a large number of politically conscious leaders locked up in deep freeze, in supermaximum security units that are the "prisons within the prisons." This is where you find the history of the Black Panther Party in the USA, and the history of Robert Hillary King, Herman Wallace and Albert Woodfox.

Whether or not you agree with the dramatic tactics of the Black Panther Party (BPP), it is important to understand that their real offense against the state was going public with the truth about this country failing in its social responsibility. Their famous ten-point program began with the demand for "power to determine the destiny of our Black and oppressed communities' education." It demanded free health care for all Black and oppressed people, an immediate end to police brutality, an immediate end to all wars of aggression, full employment, decent housing and decent education for all Black and oppressed people, freedom for all Black and oppressed people now held in U.S. Federal, state, county, city and military prisons and jails, and trials by a jury of peers. The BPP's ten-point program inspired a Free Breakfast for Children Program, free medical clinics, transportation to prisons located far from population centers for family members of inmates, community schools, and testing for sickle-cell disease. The Black Panther Party became the symbol of liberation to a generation who were questioning social contradictions.

Robert Hillary King joined the Black Panther Party while incarcerated as a young man; he tells of doing so because the party's positions and activism fit his own perspective about what was wrong with our society and what needed to be done. When Robert joined the BPP, I was serving as physician for their Bunchy Carter Free Clinic in South Central Los Angeles. As nationwide attacks on the BPP and mass arrests of its members occurred, I began to investigate the plight of my patients who had been taken off to jail. I became a forensic psychiatric "expert," explaining to judges and juries the dreadful consequences of inhuman conditions within the jails and prisons. Of course, I was an "outside expert," living in the community while touring correctional facilities and testifying in court. Robert Hillary King was learning about the same problems first hand, as a captive, and the occupant of a prison cell where he was confined for over thirty years.

In the early 1970's Herman Wallace and Albert Woodfox founded a chapter of the Black Panther Party at Angola State Prison, formerly a slave plantation. Robert joined them in their political activism within the prison, becoming a member of the first chapter of the Black Panther Party actually formed within a prison.

Community service in prison is different than in the community. Education is still a primary function, serving to bolster prisoners' sense of themselves as decent people who retain rights in spite of their incarceration. But there are other issues, unique to the prison setting. One special problem in prison is sexual victimization, rape, forced sex, and even prostitution rings where weaker prisoners are forced to provide sexual favors while their pimps receive payment. The Angola Black Panther Party organized prisoners to stamp out prostitution and sexual victimization at Angola. They also organized prisoner strikes to improve inhuman living conditions. In the process, as they stood tall and encouraged other prisoners to do likewise, their keepers felt intimidated.

The Warden at Angola State Prison, Burl Cain, would testify years later in federal court in the Angola 3's civil lawsuit to gain release from extended solitary confinement: "It's not obvious that they should be let out of extended lockdown, they were 'not good men,' they 'haven't reformed their political beliefs,' and would be disruptive to the prison environment." The Warden provides an excellent definition of a political prisoner: someone who has not reformed their political beliefs. The Warden has a right to his private views, but when he uses the occasion of a guard's murder and no clear suspect to frame prisoners whose standing tall most intimidates him, he is violating all the rights and requirements of a democracy.

Robert Hillary King was a truth-teller from very early in his life, and his touching autobiography is a page-turner. Not only the humble story of a hero in his own words, it is also a beautifully written piece of literature. A childhood in the South comes alive in the telling, the suspense mounts as the pages go by. Robert first went to jail at eighteen. In his early twenties, he was arrested for a robbery he had not done. While on trial, the man who had falsely identified Robert as his accomplice admitted his lie in court and explained that he had had to identify someone in order to get a lighter sentence. He stated to judge and jury that Robert looked nothing like the much older man who had been his partner in the robbery. He had therefore believed the other witnesses would never identify Robert, and that all charges against him would have to be dropped. In spite of the confession, Robert was still convicted as the accomplice. The court was not interested in hearing the truth, only in sending another young Black man to prison. Robert was forced to suffer the resulting disillusionment in a jail cell.

He joined the Black Panther Party in prison. He believed in the good works of the Panthers, and the need to make an impassioned statement about the scars of slavery and inequality that run deep in the American psyche. As an intellectual and a leader he was framed for the murder of an inmate, and went to "the hole," or segregation, where he remained for twenty-nine of the thirty-one years of his prison term. His fellow organizers and Black Panther Party members Herbert Wallace and Albert Woodfox were framed for a second murder: that of a guard named Brent Miller. Together they became known as the Angola 3.

A strong national campaign has been waged to free the Angola 3. The struggle has been victorious to an impressive extent. Robert was essentially exonerated (he had to plead to a lesser charge) and released from prison in 2001. Due to Robert Hillary King's activism and the National Coalition to free the Angola 3, and some excellent lawyering, the state was recently ordered by a federal court to release Herman Wallace and Albert Woodfox from segregation — but they remain in prison, and Robert is committed to winning their freedom.

The entire point of supermaximum confinement is to "break" the prisoners who are forced to reside therein. The planners hoped that prisoners would eventually emerge from segregation with their tempers calmed and their behaviors shaped into total conformity. The hope is misplaced. Many prisoners in supermaximum cells have told me that their anger mounts while inside of them, and they get frightened that they will be unable to control it. As one prisoner in a supermax prison cell recently said: "You get angry, and then you get angrier, and then you become frightened that the large anger you feel all the time will burst out and get you in more trouble, so you'll have to do more time in the hole."

Vengeance is not the answer. It's certainly an understandable personal feeling, but a poor guide to activism and social policy. Getting angry, and getting back at the people who caused one's pain and misery leads only to more pain and misery. A progressive politics created out of vengeance is not progressive. This was Nelson Mandela's great insight, and the reason he established the Truth and Reconciliation Commission after the fall of Apartheid in South Africa.

Robert Hillary King is not especially angry, even with those who falsely prosecuted and persecuted him. Robert Hillary King is a humble man, a visionary leader, and a powerful writer. In this book, he speaks frankly about the pain of living with disenfranchisement, wrongful conviction and torture in prison. But he also tells of the sweet and poignant moments in his life, of a family's love, of tender relationships, of family tragedies. His book is an indictment of the hypocrisy of a democracy that ignores the needs of a large segment of its population and then makes every attempt to disappear the evidence by locking up the people most harmed by society's callousness. But Robert Hillary King will not be disappeared. And that is why his message is so powerful and important.

Terry A. Kupers, M.D., M.S.P.
AUGUST, 2008

Terry A. Kupers, M.D., M.S.P. is Institute Professor at The Wright Institute, a Distinguished Life Fellow of the American Psychiatric Association. Besides practicing psychiatry at his office in Oakland, he consults to various public mental health centers and jail mental health services. He provides expert testimony as well as consultation and staff training regarding the psychological effects of prison conditions including isolated confinement in supermaximum security units, the quality of correctional mental health care, and the effects of sexual abuse in correctional settings. He has served as consultant to the U.S. Department of Justice, Civil Rights Division, as well as to Human Rights Watch and Amnesty International. Dr. Kupers has published extensively, including the books *Prison Madness: The Mental Health Crisis Behind Bars and What We Must Do About It* (1999) and *Public Therapy: The Practice of Psychotherapy in the Public Mental Health Clinic (1981)*. He is co-editor of *Prison Masculinities* (2002). He is a Contributing Editor of *Correctional Mental Health Report*, and received the Exemplary Psychiatrist award from the National Alliance on Mental Illness (NAMI) at the American Psychiatric Association meeting in 2005.

A WORD

I WAS BORN IN THE U.S.A. BORN BLACK, born poor. Is it then any wonder that I have spent most of my life in prison?

PREFACE

IN FEBRUARY, 1970, I WAS ARRESTED, charged, and convicted for an armed robbery which I hadn't committed. My initial sentence was thirty-five years at hard labor in the Louisiana State Penitentiary, Angola. While being held at the New Orleans Parish Prison, I escaped, and was given an additional eight years for the "aggravation" I had caused my keepers. By 1974, in addition to the forty-three years (now housed at the State Prison), I had a life sentence without the possibility of parole, probation or the suspension of sentence for allegedly having participated in the death of another prisoner. Thus, the idea to write was born. If an epitaph was to be written for me, I wanted it to be written *by* me . . .

Given that life and politics are inseparable in America, I wished to describe the events of my childhood and adult life, and draw their political conclusions. While there has been a slight alteration in my status now that I have been released from the bondage of a prison cell, I note that there has been no structural change in those institutions in society that foster racism, classism, bigotry, oppression, and disenfranchisement. After enduring solitary confinement for twenty-nine of the thirty-one years of my incarceration, my status continues, and so does my struggle.

For the sake of clarity, the reader needs to be informed of this: my given name at birth was not Robert King Wilkerson. The name given to me at birth was Robert Hillary King. I learned of this when I applied for my birth certificate on February 10th, 2001, two days after my release from Angola Prison. However, by whichever name I am called, I honor the surnames of both my parents.

At the same time, I discovered that I actually entered this existence on May 30, 1942, and that my birthday was not the third of May as I had always believed. It could very well be said that I was really born in February, 1970, when an unjust conviction and incarceration would change me forever, launching me into a new birth. But I shall begin at the beginning.

CHAPTER 1

WHEN I MET MY FATHER, HILLARY Wilkerson, for the first time I was thirteen years old. By that time, having lived an unsheltered lifestyle, I had already undergone the transition from man-child to man. But my maturity to actual manhood was to unfold more gradually. In the pages that follow, I share this unfolding with the reader.

Two young people: Male and female . . . a dark night, desire to escape and explore the unknown. Hormones working over time, helped by a nip from an hidden bottle. Nine months later (more or less), on Sunday, May 30, 1942, into this world came one Robert Hillary King — a.k.a. Robert King Wilkerson.

Hillary Wilkerson, my father — of whose seed I am the product — having experienced the joy of planting the seed, found that joy to be short-lived. In the typical fashion of many Black men of that era, he split. The responsibility for and to the product of his seed proved much more than he was willing and perhaps capable of enduring. He had to seek refuge. Hillary enlisted in the imperialist army of these United States. From there, he went on to plant seeds in other, foreign soils . . .

Clara Mae King, my mother, who was very young when my older sister, Mary, was conceived — and not much older at my own conception — never developed a true sense of responsibility toward any of the three children she eventually brought into this world. Years later, Clara would tell me that at the time of Mary's birth — and mine — she felt we would fare better with her mother, Alice, than with her. My mother was very short, and her diminutive size seemed to have played a role in shaping her personality. Clara never revealed to me directly that she had hang-ups about her size, but when I came to know her years later, I could sense the insecurity that plagued her. She began drinking alcohol at a very early age, and it was alcohol that contributed to her early death at the age of forty-one.

The first-born of my mother was Mary, two years, three months and seven days my senior. Mary took after Clara in size, inheriting the gene that prevented her growth. She also began drinking heavily, and she too died young at the age of twenty-seven.

Ella Mae, my younger sister, was born a few years after me. I didn't have the pleasure of meeting her until I was twenty-three, at my mother's wake and funeral in 1966. And it was shortly thereafter that Mary died also . . .

In retrospect, when I think of my mother Clara, I am grateful that in her attempt to shield and protect me from the savage forces that confronted her, she passed me on to her own mother, Alice. My grandmother's own standing, in many ways, was as bare as Clara's. But my grandmother did not view me (or my sister) as being a burden. And I can truthfully say that there were many other Black women of the same era who, while facing equally (or surpassing) bad odds as Clara, met the situation head on. Alice, whom I learned to call Mama, was one such woman.

At the time of my grandmother's acceptance of Mary and me, Ella wasn't born. When she was, she stayed in New Orleans. Though Mary and I were born in New Orleans, during our infancy, Clara had brought us both back to Gonzales, Louisiana, where Alice lived. Ella Mae never came to Gonzales. Shortly after her birth, Clara passed her off to another relative. However, had Clara brought Ella to Gonzales as she had done with her other two children, Mama would have also been responsible for Ella's childhood survival. That was the type of woman Mama was.

CHAPTER 2

I HAVE SOME VIVID MEMORIES OF THE WAY Gonzales was back then. There wasn't anything impressive about this small town and economic security was nearly non-existent, especially for Blacks. In order to feed her children, Mama worked the sugar cane fields, which was seasonal. I often heard her say, "I had to cut cane with ice on the stalks." They grew a lot of corn there also. The town's school was known by the simple name of "Smith's." I never knew the name of the school for whites. I remember Orice's Grocery, where Mama used to "deal" ("dealing" was synonymous with having established credit). Orice's memory is vivid because, whenever I went there with Mama, I was always treated to a "moonshine cookie," so called because of its size and shape. My great grandparents also lived in Gonzalez, as well as some of my great uncles and cousins.

Gonzalez's jailor, part-time handyman, and part time janitor, was Black. According to Mama, the man who wore all of these titles was a distant cousin of ours. One day we stopped by the jail while this cousin was in the process of dining. The very first thing I noticed about him was that he had only one arm. He tried his damnedest to get me to join with him in his eats, offering me the same utensil he was eating from. I just stared at him. The truth is, I didn't want any of that food. And the reason was, in the corner was another Black man, behind what I then described as being a "lot of skinny iron." From behind this iron, the man watched us all, somber-like. Looking into his face, I immediately felt some kinship with him, more than with my cousin and I felt that the one-armed man was responsible for keeping the somber-looking man behind that skinny iron. The one arm, too, I found at that age to be monstrous. I disliked our cousin, and I was glad when we left.

When we had gone some distance, I asked Mama what that other man was doing at our cousin's house, and why was he behind all that skinny iron? She told me that it wasn't our cousin's house, but a jailhouse, that our cousin only worked there. And she told me that the man behind the *bars* (not skinny iron) must have done something bad to be there. She called him a "cornvick." I was only about four years old at the time, and my small mind went to work. It told me that since there were many cornfields around, a "cornvick" must live between the stalks and was considered "bad" for doing so.

I was glad we lived in a house. It was an old, decrepit house, just off of the highway. It was shabby, unpainted, and leaky; whenever it rained, that old house rained also. The summers weren't too bad, our house had lots of holes in it which served as air ducts. But the winters, even in Louisiana, were bitterly cold. At that time, Mama had nine living children of her own: Clara, my birth mother, was the eldest; Robert and Ruth were fraternal twins; Houston was next in line. Then there were George, Henry, William, Verna Mae, and James. By the time I made my fifth birthday, Clara, Robert, Ruth, Houston, George, and Henry (whom Mama had called her "first set of children") had all gone their respective ways, some leaving as young as thirteen years old. That left William, Verna Mae, James, Mary and me, and of course, Mama.

One bright summer evening, before Houston and George departed, I remember standing in our yard, looking across the street at the well-painted houses with manicured lawns inhabited by whites. I saw some activity in one of those yards. Looking closer, I saw two of my uncles, Houston and George, in a row of pear trees, loaded with ripened fruits. Houston and George were violently shaking the trees, while nearby a dog barked incessantly. When they would get through shaking one tree, they would rush to another, repeating the effort.

After doing this a number of times, they began picking the fallen pears from the ground and throwing them across the street, into our yard. Everywhere I looked, it seemed to be raining fruit. I wanted desperately to pick one up and eat it, but each time I attempted this, falling pears would barely miss my head. I began to dart from place to place, but everywhere I darted, more pears fell. Soon the thought of trying to get a pear left me. I was now desperate for some shelter. I tried to make it to the porch and into the house for safety, but the falling pears cut me off. So I just stood there, rooted in one place, and began to holler, louder and louder. I think my loud bellowing actually scared my uncles. I know for sure that it got their attention. They stopped throwing and began gesturing wildly for one of the other children to usher me to safety.

When George and Houston returned from that escapade, we all had a big laugh. It was not long after this incident that George and Houston departed from us, only to be seen again years down the road.

With the departure of Houston and George and with Mama working six days a week, the responsibility to watch us when Mama wasn't home fell to William, the next oldest. Each day after Mama left for work, we would find ourselves plagued by a huge German shepherd dog that belonged to one of the whites living across the street. That dog *knew* we were alone, and that we were afraid of it. We would all be out in the yard playing, and one of the children would see it coming and yell, "Here comes the dog, git on the roof!" That was the safest place to hide from the dog when Mama wasn't around. We had to shinny up a post to get to the roof, and as the littlest, I was always last. William would always be the one to reach down and pull me to safety.

One day everyone was too busy playing to keep much of an eye out for the dog. By the time we spotted the animal, it had advanced too near. Everyone broke into a dead run straight for the porch. First William, then Verna, now Mary, then James. By the time James had shinnied up the post, the shepherd was on the porch, snarling and baring its fangs. I tried to wrap my little legs around the post, at the same time reaching toward William, who was yelling for me to grasp his outstretched hand. At one point, William had me in his grasp. But then I slipped: I fell hard.

Thinking only of the dog, I immediately sprang to my feet, turning around to face it. By this time, it was right upon me. I was trapped and I wasn't expecting any help from William or any of the rest of them. They had proven time and time again that they were not going to tackle that dog, and neither was I! Trapped and frightened, I began to yell bloody murder. Then a strange, but wonderful, thing happened. The dog stopped in its tracks. It gave me a most curious look, dropped its tail between its legs, and hauled ass away from the premises, and didn't look back until it had reached the other side of the highway.

From that day on, I cannot recall our having any further trouble with that dog. Once more, my holler had come to my rescue!

CHAPTER 3

WILLIAM HAD LEARNED THE RUDIMENTS OF cooking, but sometimes we had nothing. On these days, we had to wait until Mama came home. We all found consolation in sight of her coming up the highway, grocery bags in arms.

On one of those days, knowing that we all were hungry, she headed straight to the kitchen to prepare a meal. I was right behind her, holding onto her skirt. Every now and then she would reach down to cuddle me, saying, "Don't worry, baby, mama gon' feed you in a little while." And I was believing this, too. I really thought it would only be a "little while." But a "little while" turned into a "huge while" that to a kid could seem like forever. Every now and then Mama would lift a lid from one of the pots, and the smell escaping would assault me with such intensity that I would bend over, holding my arm across my empty belly. Each time she would do it, Mama would say, "Just a little longer, children," or something to that effect. Finally I could stand it no longer. She lifted a lid from one of the pots, and before she could say a word my belly growled in protest, and I followed suit: I started hollering and bellowing and didn't stop until she knelt down and took me in her arms. It was this soul-searing yelling and bellowing that made Mama realize how truly hungry I was. She said, "Oh, my poor baby!" The rice was already done. The meats in the pots were not quite done, but the gravy was. I eagerly ate rice and gravy . . .

I have related these childhood incidents because I feel there is a present-day application that can be drawn from them. The application is: when one has a legitimate beef, a loud protest is the correct behavior.

Later I remember a deluge: Water — seemingly with a desire for retribution — literally poured from the sky. And the water rose. More than three feet high, it covered our porch and beyond. Inside the house the water was nearly up to my knees; off the porch, the water would be over my head.

The morning after the rain ceased, Mama had to wade in water up to her waist in order to get to the highway so she could proceed to work. The land on our side of the highway was much lower than the other side, where the whites lived.

Before Mama left that morning, she told William to keep us all inside, and for him to stay there too. But as soon as Mama was out of sight, William was heading for the porch. We all followed him. I stopped in the middle of the porch, for William told me to stay where I was. He and the others went splashing off into the yard. Watching them play, I felt alone, and the farther away they waded, the more alone I felt. I began to inch my way towards the end of the porch. I really didn't intend to go off the porch, but with my eyes trained on their retreating forms, the spell was cast. Each time they would take a step, I would take one. The water did the rest. It was polite enough to pull me right off the edge of the porch. This is one time my yelling failed me. I tried, but nothing, not a sound would escape from my mouth. Then, from what seemed like a mile away, I heard Mary yelling: "Oh look! Junior is drowning, Junior is drowning." They all hurried back as fast as they could, and pulled me to safety. I was numb with fear, but most grateful. I remember hearing William say: "We ain't goin' tell Mama about this, y'all hear?"

Mama never found out.

A few days later — the water now receded — we were out playing once more. We spotted a big fat field rat. William decided to tackle it. He found a stick, and advanced upon the creature, backing it into a corner. Having no place to turn, the rat went on the offensive. It leapt up and caught one of William's fingers, biting down viciously. Surprisingly, William didn't scream. Instead, he seized the rat by the throat, and choked it to death. When he pried its mouth open his finger looked as if it had been torn by a pair of pliers.

We all went back to the house, bringing the dead rat with us. William poured coal oil on his wounded finger, which stopped the bleeding. Then he found a spider-web and wrapped it around his finger. He poured more coal oil on the web and finger, and wrapped a clean rag around it. The finger seemed to take no time to heal . . .

As for the rat, well . . . after dressing his finger, William put on a pot of water to boil. While the water was boiling, he reached for a kitchen knife and handed it to Verna, who gutted and cleaned the rat. The boiling water was used to make a rat stew, which we obligingly ate for lunch. After that day, William became somewhat of a hero to me, someone I could look up to. I was four years old at the time.

With school beginning, and the rest of the children away, Mama would bring me to her parents' house, and they would mind me while she worked.

Alice's parents, Robert and Mary Larks, were my great grandparents, whom I addressed as "Grandpa" and "Grandma." I am told that they had a total of twelve children, but in my lifetime I've only met seven: Norsey and Morris were the males; Carrie, Alice, Clementine, Alma and Alka were the females.

With all of their children grown and gone, Grandpa and Grandma had lots of free time, and in their leisure, they were glad to have me around. But they were also to be feared at all times. Whenever either of them spoke, it seemed like a command. I stood in awe of both.

I am told that they both were part African and part "Indian," that is, Native-American. Her form of disciplining was the pulling of the ears, his was the traditional "strop," as he called it. I tried to steer clear, always, of Grandpa's "strop." Neither Grandpa nor Grandma was mean or anything of the sort. They were just two people who tolerated no nonsense.

I remember once Grandpa and I were in his garden, hoeing the plants. Actually, Grandpa was doing the hoeing. Every now and then I would make an attempt at it, but the hoe I was trying to use wouldn't let me. If the hoe wasn't falling from my hands, I was falling to the ground in my attempt at hoeing! Each time this would happen, Grandpa would throw back his head and roar with laughter.

Around noontime, we left the garden and headed to the house for lunch. Grandma was out visiting at the time, so Grandpa opened the china cabinet, removed a deep dish, and began filling it with good smelling food. Thinking it was my food, I was ready to sit and eat. But Grandpa sat at the table and began to eat all by himself instead. I stood there watching him all the while, wondering just when he would fix mine. When Grandpa had eaten all but a little of the food, he got up, nudged me to his chair, and told me to eat the rest. I sat eagerly and ate what was left.

That evening Mama came and picked me up. She asked me, "What did you and papa do today?" I told her that we had worked in his garden, and that afterwards, Grandpa had gone into the house and fixed himself a great big plate of food. I motioned with my arms to show what a great big plate of food it was. Mama asked "Well, did he fix you one too?" I said, "No, Mama, he didn't fix me no plate."

Mama was really asking if had I eaten that day. But at the time, my child's rationale could not understand this. I answered directly, and what I thought to be correctly. Grandpa hadn't fixed me a dish when he had fixed his own. But the way it came out, Mama believed that Grandpa hadn't fed me at all.

The next day, when Mama dropped me off at Grandpa's, she turned to him and went into an unexpected tirade. "My baby tells me that y'all worked in the garden yesterday and afterwards, y'all went into the house and fixed you food, but you didn't feed him." She went on, "I leave my baby here with y'all, and if you don't feed him, Papa, how do you expect him to eat?" At her words my ears perked up, because I hadn't said Grandpa didn't feed me, I had just said he hadn't fixed me a plate! But wisely,

I kept my mouth shut. By Grandpa's logic I had already lied on him, and if I had said anything, Mama would have interpreted that as me calling her a liar too. Grandpa's mouth flew wide open; he was beyond just angry. He began to stutter, his face started twitching, and large veins protruded from his neck. I remember it from all those years ago because I learned then that even telling the truth can be misunderstood, and it can be the root of miscommunication.

For the rest of the morning, I made it a point to follow Grandpa around the house. In my little mind, I was doing my best to appease him. But whenever I'd get too close to him, he'd yell, "Git out of the way!" to let me know he would not be appeased. I could hear him mumbling to himself: " . . . telling your Ma I didn't feed you huh? I'm gon' fix ya." But Grandpa never did "fix" me. Instead, around noontime, we went back into the kitchen where he ordered me to sit down at the table. He then reached into the china cabinet and extracted the same dish as the previous day. He filled it up with food and set it in front of me, saying, "Now lie and tell your Ma I didn't feed you again, you hear!"

CHAPTER 4

SINCE MAMA'S LIFE AND MINE ARE intertwined, and since this autobiography could not be written with any degree of accuracy — or for that matter could not have been written at all, but for her — I think it is appropriate here to pause and delve briefly into the history of one Alice King, and the troubles she faced.

Mama and her husband, "Mr. King," had gone their separate ways long before I entered this existence, leaving Alice with seven children to raise on her own — and two more children coming later on. With her first six children coming prior to, and immediately following, the 1929 crash of the stock market, ushering in the Great Depression that lasted throughout the 1930s — it was pure hell for her back then.

Mama worked the sugar cane fields from sun up 'til sun down for less than a dollar a day. During the off-season, she washed, ironed clothes, and scrubbed floors for whites for pennies a day or for left-over food. Her bunions and blisters told a bitter but vivid tale of her travails. But with all the scars for show, her economic status was nil. In fact, this status for Black folks and poor whites was normal, but more so for Blacks. Racism, discrimination, and prejudice were rampant throughout America.

The thing that stood out most in her character was her quiet, unselfish spirit and her ability to endure without complaints. Being long-suffering, she was content with her meager state of existence. She never really, deeply, questioned anything. In the final analysis, everything accorded her was God's will. She bore her suffering and repression stoically. She never lost the belief that she would later be rewarded for her trials here on earth in a city whose streets were paved with gold. This was her only solace, though her trials were many.

When considering Mama's own state of hardship, I have to also view it in light of the other twenty-five million colonial subjects of the era. If distress and suffering could be measured in terms of weight, the distress and the suffering of Blacks in America could sink a million Titanics.

Following the crash of the stock market, there arose a lot of grumbling among people in general. Dissent, among the "privileged race" as well as Blacks, prompted a few reforms and other governmental concessions, such as welfare.

Then, with the coming of World War II, industry was once more on the rise. The job market increased, and Black leaders threatened to march on the White House unless they got some of the jobs being given out. As a result, President Franklin Roosevelt signed executive orders, opening the doors for Black subjects to enter into industry. However, as it turned out, only a few Blacks were lucky enough to acquire good paying jobs. Discrimination in the job market and racism were still rampant, and the vast majority of Blacks were still jobless.

Such were the conditions to which Mama had to conform, and which made her lifestyle one of distress and suffering. And this lifestyle extended throughout the 1930s and well into the 1940s.

At four and a half years of age, my ears didn't miss much. One day when Mama came to pick me up, I heard Grandma say: "Monk, you are going to work yourself to death. Why don't you get on relief"? (Monk had been her childhood name.) So ultimately, Mama, with most of her first set of children grown and gone their separate ways, and still confronted with grief and distress, decided to take refuge in "relief" (i.e. welfare) as a means to supplement her meager income.

After getting on relief, things got a little better. Mama still worked, though. We finally moved from that old house on Airline Highway, where the floods came frequently, inundating the house during the summers, bringing snakes in abundance and where, during the winter months, she would have to place old overcoats over our thin covers in an effort just to keep us warm.

With the new house came a dog, a big German shepherd we called Ring, short for Ringer. Ring was a pretty smart dog, and he'd do more than what was expected of him. Sometimes he would follow us into the woods, leave us, and go off to hunt. He would capture rabbits, squirrels, turtles, opossums, armadillos and even snakes. Not only would Ring bring game back from his hunt, he was good at "finding" other things: clothes and shoes — he was even smart enough to get the shoes in pairs!

Then one day, without warning, Ring went mad. William, James, and I were preparing to go into the woods, but Ring was nowhere in sight. We began yelling for him, but got no response. Then James found Ring underneath the house.

After taking one glance at the dog, I knew something was wrong. Ring had a fierce glare in his eyes: his teeth were bared, and he was slobbering all over the place. James, not understanding the vast difference between the Ring of other days and of that day, reached in after him. Ring sprang, sinking his fangs into James's arm. At this point, we all broke into a dead run, straight for the porch stairs. By this time, Mama and the others had heard the commotion and run out to see what all the fuss was about. Panting and frightened, we told her all that had happened. James's bloody arm was the evidence.

Our cousin Chest (short for Chester) was visiting that day. He appeared outside, rifle in hand. Ring had gone back underneath the house, and was peering out in a curious manner: his eyes still glowed. Chest went over, and after taking one look at Ring, concluded that the dog had "gone mad." In retrospect, I don't really think Ring was mad, because he seemed to have a remorseful look in his eye, as if he instinctively knew he had done something wrong. But at the time, I did think Ring was mad, and like the rest of the children, I stayed back, out of the way.

Cousin Chest approached closer to the dog, and in a loud commanding voice, he said, "Come 'ere, Ring!" And Ring, without the slightest hesitation came out from under the house with his head bowed in submission. Again, in retrospect, I think that Ring's instinct told him he would die that day.

When Chest raised the rifle and took aim, Ring raised his head, looked briefly at each of us as if to apologize, then as a last and final gesture, Ring dropped his head in a complete form of surrender. The rifle cracked and Ring fell dead, shot through the head. We all cried.

It was later rumored that some whites who wanted Ring, but couldn't have him, decided to make sure that no one else kept him. Still later, another rumor surfaced, which was that people knew that the dog was stealing their clothes and other items, and decided to eliminate him by poisoning him. While both of these rumors sound plausible, the latter seems more believable.

About a week or so later, we were all seated around the large fireplace in the house, enjoying the warmth, when all of a sudden James broke into a run, straight for the fire! He was caught and held just before reaching the flames. Looking at him was just like looking at Ring all over again. His eyes seemed to have receded into his head. He had the same vacant stare, and he was foaming at the mouth, making deep guttural sounds. Mama had to place a spoon in his mouth to keep him from swallowing his tongue. James was brought to the doctor, and from that day on, it was said that James had "spells" resulting from his having been bitten by Ring. When we moved to New Orleans, James's spells were later diagnosed as epilepsy by doctors. Nevertheless, the family still clung to the idea that James's seizures resulted from the incident with the dog.

It was soon time for Mama to send me to school. I was big for my age, not quite six years old. And I was eager to join the rest of the children. I did reasonably as a first grader. At the end of the year, however, school officials decided not to pass me on to the second grade. The reason given was that I was too young. I often wondered later, had I been white and affluent, would they have allowed me to move ahead, and encouraged whatever potential I may have had?

Shortly after my fifth year in existence, I became aware of my uncle, Robert King — whom I was named after. Robert had begun to show up periodically at the house with his "wives." He was the oldest son of Mama, the first to leave home. Each time he came home with a "wife," we children would immediately adopt her into the family, calling her "sister."

One day Robert came to the house and told Mama that he had finally "settled down" — that he was living in New Orleans, on the west bank, in the area known as Algiers. He tried and finally convinced Mama to move to Algiers, where some of her children lived.

The day we moved, Robert came with one of his male friends in a large, open-bodied truck. We piled in all of our belongings and headed for New Orleans, Louisiana, the place where I was born. While the move to New Orleans was significant, it was nothing compared to the friend that my uncle had brought with him. I didn't know it at the time, but that man would play a most important role in my life.

CHAPTER 5

MORE THAN THE GREAT MUDDY Mississippi River separated New Orleans's east side from the west side, also known as Algiers. While Algiers sported its own downtown district, its own police precinct, and even a small loading dock, it was considered rural and unsophisticated in comparison to its urban counterpart across the river, which was known by a variety of names: The Crescent City, The Big Easy, and Greater New Orleans, to name a few. New Orleans (east) was a growing metropolis, reeking with an energetic frenzy, making the separation psychological as well as physical. But Algiers suited Mama just fine, in spite of the fact that three of her sisters (Clementine, Alma, and Alka) all resided in New Orleans across the river from her.

We moved into an unimpressive, brown, brick-papered house which consisted of three rooms and a kitchen, and of course, the conventional outhouse. It wasn't like the house in Gonzales — we were surrounded by other houses, taking away some of the emptiness. Algiers promised gaiety and liveliness, too: there was even a barroom next door.

After "Mr. King," Mama never remarried. Now in her forties — and nine children later — she was still relatively attractive, so she had no trouble being seen and "found" by another man who cared. That man was Robert "Mule" Manning. He was the friend who had come with my uncle to help us to move. I immediately took to Mule and, as the saying goes, "I colored him father."

His nickname, "Mule," was put on him by some of his cronies who worked with him. Whenever there was work, Mule never missed a day. The type of work he did wasn't year-round; it consisted of loading sugar into boxcars for shipment to different places around the country. Other times, he did carpentry, masonry, or whatever it took to make a dollar honestly. Mule didn't make a lot of money, but whatever money he made, his new family came first. It is to Mule that I owe part of my childhood survival.

Originally from the state of Georgia, Mule had traveled all over the country, mostly by freight trains: yes, he was a one-time hobo. He eventually told me about a lot of his hobo adventures, and years later, one of his stories would help me through a very tough situation.

Mule was divorced from his wife. The marriage had produced two children, a boy and a girl. Both by this time were grown. Mule took an instant liking to all of Mama's children. He and I spent a lot of time together, and we became real attached to each other. Mule had a unique way of adding humor to nearly everything he did. For instance, he loved to drink wine, and his favorite was muscatel, but he called it muscat, because of the smell it left on the breath. He would produce a pint bottle from his back pocket, turn it around to the clear side, and hold it up to the light so that the label on the opposite side could be seen. He would then tell me to call out the letters backwards. I'd say, "l-e-t-a-c-s-u-m." He would ask me, "Do you know what that says?" I would shake my head, and he would say, "Don't you get it, sport? Let's act some!" He would then go through the ritual of carefully opening the bottle, taking a long drink, and after recapping it, putting it back in his pocket as carefully as he had removed it. To Mule, and others of his day, "Let's act some," meant the same as acting up, or creating a disturbance. Mule never acted up though, and the only thing the wine did for him was wind him up to talk about his past experiences, which we would all enjoy.

At some point during my fifth year in existence, my level of cognition expanded from a mere perceptual observation to a degree of conceptual recognition. It was not just memory; I was beginning to be able to form patterns, and add ideas to those things I encountered. It happened so quickly and unexpectedly; it was as if I'd awakened one day into a new world, both beautiful and mysterious. I was full of life. And being full of life, I wanted very much to partake of this newly discovered existence.

Around this same time, I was out playing with some of the other children from the neighborhood when I noticed doors beginning to pop open, windows going up; people were coming out onto their porches, pointing at someone coming down the street, a stranger. I stopped playing and looked also. I saw a little girl and wondered what was so uncommon about a little girl walking down the street. But taking a closer look, I saw that what I had thought to be a little girl was actually a full-grown woman, fewer than four feet tall. By this time, she had advanced to where I was playing with the other kids; a small crowd of grown-ups and children had followed her.

The lady asked no one in particular, "Is this Le Boeuf Street?" Someone volunteered that it was. The lady then asked, "Do any body know where Miss King lives?" When I heard her inquiring about Mama, this really got my attention, and I wanted to answer her, but someone in the crowd said, "There's one of Miss King's sons," pointing at me. The little lady turned toward me, looking me up and down, as if trying to discern who I was. She smiled, then said, "Baby, can you take me to your mama?"

"Yes, ma'am," I said. Mama was sitting on the porch when we approached. The lady saw Mama and began to smile, and Mama, with a look of instant recognition and delight, smiled back at the lady and said, "Lord, here comes Clara Mae!" Then she turned to me: "Boy, Junior, here is your mama." This was in 1948, some three months prior to my sixth year in existence.

Up to that point, I had no idea that Clara, my biological mother, existed. And whether or not it was Clara's purpose to take Mary and me with her, I cannot say. But I do know that Mama would never have permitted it. So Clara's visit only established the fact, that she, not Mama, was my "real" mother and that Alice, whom I called Mama, was actually my maternal grandmother. When Alice said "Boy . . . here is your mama" it sounded strange and incomprehensible. And it remained strange, for Alice was "Mama" until the day she died, and Clara Mae, despite the love that eventually grew in me for her, remained Clara Mae until the day she died.

The move to New Orleans afforded Mama the privilege of being near three of her grown children: Clara, Robert, and his twin sister, Ruth. This close proximity brought some comfort to her. Shortly after our arrival, my uncle Houston had made a showing, but had since departed again. At this point, Mama had no idea where Houston, George, or Henry were. Clara, who had made her retreat as boldly and as unexpectedly as she had come, lived somewhere uptown, across the river, but I didn't see her again until I was nearly twelve years old. Robert and Ruth lived only a short distance from where we lived, and both visited regularly. It was during this period that I first became conscious of Ruth, who Mama always said was her "best child."

I was in grade school, and during this period, it was never boring. In school, a whole new world opened to me: I met a lot of new faces, and made a lot of new friends. The girls in my classes fascinated and intrigued me. I was infatuated with most of them. I cannot begin to count the number of girls or the number of times I fell secretly in love. And whether I was reciting lessons in class, fighting other boys, swimming or whatever, I felt I was able to do it better because I knew some girl was watching. Years later, I came to the conclusion that those first few years in school were the height of my receptive stage, and that I was only absorbing higher images and impressions of the external world known as nature. Nature had cast me just beyond the threshold of the first stage of cognition, and I was making the leap from the first to the second stage: from external to internal, from quantitative to qualitative. The fascination and whatever else I may have felt about nature's objects in my path — including girls — was only a feedback of a higher form of nature at work upon my then totally receptive brain cells. But at the time, I didn't know how to define or handle this. Thus, the development of an ego. While in grade school, I became a little show-off in front of my classmates, especially those of the opposite sex.

On a visit to Grandma (really my great-grandmother, of course), I learned two things: one was not to interfere when grown-ups were talking. It was her 70th birthday and we had all gone back to Gonzales to celebrate it with her. While cutting her cake, she paused and entered into what I thought was too long a conversation with another relative. Impatiently, I said, "Grandma, I ain't had no cake yet." Grandma stopped talking, a look of quiet rage on her face. She grabbed my left ear, yanking down hard, and said, "Don't you interfere when grown-ups are talking." She continued: "I know your number and it ain't come up yet. Now be quiet!" And quiet I was.

The second thing I learned on that visit to Grandma was that Mama's former husband, Henry King Sr., or "Mr. King" as she called him, had died. I often wondered why Mama had addressed her husband as "mister," and I asked her. She told me that when she had married, she was very young and that her husband was almost twenty years older than her. So she always called him "mister." I guess I can understand Mama's logic. After all, she was brought up during a period when children still respected their elders. Her learning that "Mr. King" had passed didn't seem to affect her too much. And so "Mr. King," who had never existed for me, abruptly ceased to exist for Mama as well.

In early 1949, a letter arrived from the authorities at the Michigan State Prison telling Mama that Houston was confined in their prison in Jackson, Michigan. The news that Houston was in prison hurt and haunted Mama. I think this was the very beginning of her major worries. And to compound matters, there was still no word as to the whereabouts of her other two wayward sons, George and Henry Jr.

The barroom next door was a thriving little business. It was owned by the man we rented from. On Friday and Saturday nights, the place was filled with people escaping the dullness and toil of the previous week. The juke-box kept up a continuous blast of music: the clapping of hands, laughter, and the stamping of feet could be heard in the distance. Late one weekend night, we heard a blast like thunder; someone had been shot. We later learned that the person shot was Ruth's husband, Berry, and the person doing the shooting was the proprietor, the man we rented from.

The rumor was, the man had accused Berry of owing him two cents, and Berry had refused to pay him, alleging that he had already paid the two cents. An argument ensued, and it finally ended with a shotgun blast. Luckily Berry wasn't hit with the full blast, and those few pellets that did hit him didn't penetrate any vital organs. He lived.

That weekend night was just a prelude to the many others I would witness, or hear about, where, without the slightest provocation, or hesitation, one Black subject would wound or slay another with an exaggerated intensity as if it were an act of nobility or a right of passage to manhood. And as I grew, I questioned the basis for this problem and many other problems that plague us within the colonies of America. I knew that these problems didn't exist in a vacuum, there had to be reasons. Where, I asked myself, did the root of the problems lie? And much later, after careful thought, I summarized (and here, the reader will have to bear with me, for I cannot think of a better place than here to make these valid points) as follows: brought forth in chains; stripped of humanity; deprived of culture, or most of it; taught a warped sense of values by stripping us of responsibility for each other and our off-spring; "freed" but still enslaved — a personification of these problems can be seen in colonial subjects. It takes on human form; yeah, it stalks, gropes in confusion. It self-destructs by slaying itself, committing unseeing acts against itself with all intensity, as it was programmed to do, and takes pride in its own affliction . . . Yes! Black subjects, stripped . . . degraded . . . deprived . . . demoralized . . . and psychotic-minded (resulting from past and current experiences in America) must attempt to prove their worth and their manhood, even if at the expense of each other. The causes of this effect are a trio: slavery, oppression, and racism. To label it "Black on Black" crime, or to say that the Black subject is inherently criminal, is a gross oversimplification and misrepresentation of the true facts and actual causes and this, in itself, is criminal.

CHAPTER 6

SHORTLY AFTER BERRY WAS SHOT, WE moved to another house. This house, located on Hendee Street, was much like the one we had left behind in Gonzales. In fact, the house on Hendee Street was in worse shape than the one in Gonzales. It didn't even have electricity, so one day when Mama was at work, William climbed a utility pole and ran a wire from the pole to the house. He didn't hook it up to the main line; he just wanted to make it look like we had electricity like everyone else. But if William had any thought of becoming an electrician, Mama rebuked it out of him when she got home.

One of my two most memorable events in that house on Hendee was seeing my aunt Clementine for the first time. Aunt Clem (as we called her) was a proud, impressive — and, if I may add — attractive woman. She and her husband, Uncle Willie, had come to New Orleans years earlier. They had managed to acquire a bar and restaurant, a double and single house, and several other properties. Among the properties she owned was the famous Club Rocket. Many of the old-timers knew it. It was located at the corner of Jackson and Derbigny. My first (and last) impression of Aunt Clem was that she was a very kind and compassionate person. I remember her saying to Mama, "Why don't you come over the river, and live in one of my houses?" At the time, Mama declined, but the invitation was left open. Mama was a proud, independent woman who took pride in making her own way without relying on anyone, even her relatives.

The other memorable event in the house on Hendee was my very first experience with muscatel (wine), or "Let-ac-sum," if you prefer. It occurred on a Friday. I was kept home from school for some reason or another. Mama and I were on our way to visit Ruth, who lived close by. Just before getting to Ruth's house, we spotted Mule making his way homeward. Held underneath his arm, wrapped in newspaper, was a familiar oblong shape that I knew to be a fifth of his favorite muscatel. And I had also come to know that whenever Mule had his supply of wine, money was high.

We met up with him, and while he and Mama talked, my little mind was beginning to work . . . scheming, thinking that here was a chance to get ahead of the other children, in nickels and dimes. I asked Mama could I go back home with Mule, and without hesitating, she said yes and proceeded on her journey. But just before getting out of hearing range, she turned back toward us and said, "Ba, don't you give that boy none of that wine." ("Ba" was the pet name she and Mule used when addressing each other.) Mule said, "Aw, Ba, you know I ain't gon' do nothin' like that," all the while looking at me and winking his eye. I winked back. Mama's attempt to protect me from the wine had just the opposite affect. She put it on my mind. All I had intended to do was to talk Mule out of some change. But with the wink that Mule gave me, I got the idea that I could get my very first drink of wine, too.

Just before reaching home, I went out on the limb: I asked Mule, was he really going to give me a "lil' taste," as he called it? He said, "Naw, Ba wouldn't like that." Then he added: "You can't handle it, anyway." "Whatcha mean, I can't handle it?" I said, trying to sound offended. He said, "Ba would know I gave you some, because you'd be stumbling all over the place." "No I won't," I said. For the rest of the journey home, nothing else was said about the wine. I was hopeful, because there was no note of finality in Mule's voice when he said he wouldn't give me a "lil' taste." I had sensed that he was reluctant, not because Ba had forbidden it, but only because he thought I couldn't handle it. So when we reached home I asked again, assuring him that I could handle it. Mule had himself hit the bottle several times since we reached the house, and I guess this helped him to throw caution to the wind. He poured about two fingers' worth into a cup and gave it to me. I drank it all in one gulp, smacking my lips afterwards. When the liquor reached my palate, I tasted its sweetish tinge, and almost at the same time, I experienced the tingling, burning sensation in my stomach, and the light-headedness that follows. Mule watched me down the drink, then asked me how did it taste? I said, "Good!" He asked me if I wanted some more, and of course, I assented. Mule said, "All right, I tell you what, we gon' play a little game."

The game was, I had to walk a straight line, along a board on the floor, without staggering. I had my second drink. I walked it again, and was rewarded with my third. All I could think of now was, I wanted more wine. Mule would urge me to walk a straight line, applauding me when I did, and rewarding me with more wine. At one point I heard him say to me that I was getting drunk. In a blurred voice, I assured him I wasn't. He asked me, did I think I could make it to the grocery, which was about a block and a half away? I told him I could, and he promised me another "lil' taste" when I returned. As I stepped from the house I saw that the sky was a radiant blue, not a cloud to it and it seemed as if the very sky exuded an energy that I floated on, all the way to the store. I got the items Mule wanted and started back home. About halfway there, the wine hit me hard: I began groping as one might do in a darkened room. I somehow managed to find my way home. My groping turned to stumbling, and in my hazy state I heard Mule telling me, "See, I told you that you couldn't handle it." I was totally inebriated, drunk as a skunk. In my drunken state, I saw Mule go into his pocket and take out a handful of coins and offer them to me. I held out my hand to receive them but something went wrong, and money spilled everywhere — quarters, dimes, nickels, and pennies were spread all over the floor. I dropped down on hands and knees in an effort to retrieve the coins . . . Mule began to laugh uncontrollably . . . and that's the last thing I remember . . .

I awoke the next morning about nine o'clock, with the sun beaming in on my face. Mama entered the room, and asked me how I was doing. Then she gave me a mild rebuke, saying, "Boy, I told you not to drink none of that liquor." Later, I overheard her telling Mule, "Robert, I ain't playin'. Don't you *ever* give that boy no mo' wine."

We didn't stay very long in that house on Hendee Street. We moved to Jefferson Parish, Gretna, then back to Orleans Parish, in Algiers. The Algiers house was located on Wall Boulevard, just off of Whitney Avenue. It was at this new location that Mama received another troublesome letter. This one came in reference to her other son, Henry King, Jr. He was confined in the Virginia State Prison. Like Houston's imprisonment, Henry's incarceration also haunted Mama. And still, no word from her other son, George . . .

A name can be very deceiving, sometimes. Wall Boulevard was such a name. When I think of a boulevard, what comes to mind is a wide, smooth street with beautiful trees lined up on both sides, providing shade for lovely houses. But the "boulevard" I lived on was a total antithesis to this. It was a dirt road with pot holes every few yards, and shabby shacks instead of lovely houses. Directly across the street, on the other side of the "boulevard," there was a swampy wooded area, covering about four square blocks. The whole area was scary, especially at night. And Mule didn't make it any better with his exaggerated spooky tales.

While I learned to live with Mule's spooky stories, I never learned to live with the contradiction between what the name of the street implied, and what it actually was. A lot of folks dubbed the 1950s "The Golden Years." But there were no golden days for us as a family, or for that matter, for most of America. It was not that people didn't desire to be prosperous: people labored, but the struggle to rise above poverty continued in a stalemate. Mule worked the docks, loading sugar, but the work was seasonal. He searched for, and occasionally found, odd jobs to fill out the down times. Mama still found, and worked, jobs cooking and cleaning for those whites who could afford her. Her pay was never much, but it helped. However, despite our general poverty, for about four months out of the year — the period when Mule worked steady at the docks — my little world seemed almost luxurious; there was plenty to eat; there were nickels, dimes, quarters, and even a new piece of clothing from time to time.

Mule needed his muscatel, and he always made sure he started the next morning with a "lil' taste." But sometimes his "lil' taste" ran out. So Mule devised a scheme to guard against this. There was this bar, located about four blocks from where we lived, called the Jungle Bar, perhaps because of the densely wooded area adjacent to it. Mule was never a barroom type, and he seldom went to them, but he and the owner of the Jungle Bar were friends. They had an agreement that went something like this: no matter what time of the day or night I went to the bar, the owner would know that I was on a wine errand for Mule. It didn't matter if the bar was closed; the owner and his wife always slept in the place, to sell to late customers. Many nights, mostly on week ends, Mule would awaken me and say: "Hey, Sport, you want to make a quarter?" I always knew what he wanted, and without hesitating I would tell him, yes.

Late one Friday night — or early one Saturday morning — Mule sent me on a mission to get his "lil' taste." I left the house at a dead run, and reached the bar in no time. It was after midnight, and the place was closed. I knocked on the door, and called the owner. A voice from inside, recognizing my voice, asked "What do you want, a big 'un (a quart) or a small 'un (a pint)?" "A big 'un," I said. While waiting for the owner to bring the wine, I glanced up the street, and spotted a bright set of headlights approaching. Immediately I knew it was a police car. My first impulse was to run, but after weighing the options, I stayed where I was. The car stopped and two policemen emerged. One asked, "What are you doin' out here this time o' morning, kid?" I couldn't tell him I was on a mission for Mule, so off the top of my head, I said, "This place belongs to my uncle. He asked me to come real early so that he and I can go shopping for my back-to-school clothing." By this time the owner had the wine, and was about to open the door, but had stopped when he heard voices. When he opened the door, he said, "You're too early, son. We ain't leavin' 'til 'round nine o'clock," all the while looking at the policemen and smiling. The officers smiled back, satisfied that I had told the truth; they told my "uncle" to make sure I stayed inside, and then left. My "uncle" and I had a good laugh. After waiting long enough to make sure the cops were gone, I got the wine and ran home — again at a dead run to be sure. After that episode, whenever Mule could afford it, he would give me something extra for making that particular trip.

CHAPTER. 7

IN THE LATTER PART OF 1951, THEY BEGAN clearing the large wooded area across from our house. When it was cleared, they began to build houses for Black soldiers and their families, under the G.I. Bill. It didn't take them very long to put up the houses, and by the summer of '52, there were about seventy or more new families living in the development known as "Truman's Park." What had been a desolate area was now bursting with new life and activity. I liked the new condition, for it eliminated some of the spookiness, and I was able to make lots of new friends. While the new houses were not overly fabulous, they had just enough sparkle in them to punctuate the shabbiness of the other houses, located on the other side of the boulevard, the side I lived on.

The same year that they began clearing the area for the new houses, my great-grandmother, Mary, passed away. At that age I didn't understand the full meaning and finality of death. But Mama did. It was, as she put it, "one of her greatest losses." And it was one of the losses she never recovered from.

Grandma was "waked" in Gonzales, Louisiana, at the Little Zion Baptist Church, and her remains were buried in the church's cemetery. I did not attend my great-grandmother's last rites, and I can only remember her as I last saw her, knife paused in midair, reaching over and pulling on my ear and saying, in a shrill, high voice, "I know your number, and it ain't come up yet!"

Not long after Grandma's passing, there was a strange, full-grown greyhound dog that seemingly came out of nowhere and befriended us. With no apparent owner in sight, we befriended the dog, and though Mama warned us to "Git rid of that dog, I don't like its looks!" James and I claimed ownership. One day when Mama was at one of her weekly prayer meetings, we decided to have some fun with the animal. At first the dog seemed delighted with the attention we were giving it. But James got a little carried away and wanted to straddle the dog's back for a ride through the house. The greyhound, however, would have none of this. And that's when all Hell broke loose. After taking a bite or two out of James, the hound bolted through the front door and went underneath the porch. And while the dog was making its way out the front door, I was making mine out the back. I ran as fast as I could to the church and told Mama what had happened. All she said was, "I told y'all to git rid of that dog."

When we got home, Mama washed and dressed James's inflictions, and before taking him to the hospital, got a neighbor to call the dog-catcher to come out and "take care of" the dog. I watched the official as he came and called out to the dog. The greyhound came willingly, wagging its tail in the process. The man pulled a large pistol from his holster, took quick aim, and shot the dog in the head. For me, it was like seeing the Ring episode all over again. For James, too, I guess. Up until this second incident with a dog, James's "spells" had nearly ceased altogether, but soon after this, he began to have "fit" after "fit" (as Mama called them), seemingly with a vengeance, as if to make up for lost time. He was in and out of the hospital after that. That's when the doctors told Mama that he was epileptic, and that those "fits" he was having were seizures. The doctors also predicted that the seizures would become less severe as James grew older.

Of all the bizarre things that happened while living in the house on Wall Boulevard, one stands out. It happened late one evening, not long after the incident with the greyhound. The day had been very hot and humid. Mama, as usual, was at one of her prayer services, and the rest of the children were out playing. Mule and I were sitting on the porch watching the sun as it descended deep into the western sky, and welcoming the coolness as dusk approached. At the time, there was a picket fence made out of tin that ran the length of our house, separating the house from a wooded area. I was sitting at the edge of the porch, facing the woods. From the corner of my eye, I caught sight of a small, very bright object at the far end of the fence. At first I thought it might be a spark; people in the neighborhood were always building fires to make smoke to ward off the mosquitoes. I turned completely around, to get a better view. And with seeming intelligence, the light began to travel down the length of the fence in my direction. I tried to convince myself that it was a lightning bug, but it was too bright. Mule must have sensed something, for I remember his asking me, "What are you looking at like that?" Not waiting for an answer, Mule came to the end of the porch. I continued to look, too fascinated to say anything. Mule stopped talking, and I could feel him next to me, watching. By now I was standing up. I somehow got the idea that whatever it was "knew" that it had our attention, and wanted to keep it. The light would stop, then move a few inches to the left, and then to the right, but never leaving its course along the fence. As it approached some of my fascination was replaced by fear and apprehension. I am sure Mule was experiencing the same symptoms. Nevertheless, we both continued to watch the light until it was directly across from us, only fifteen feet away, where it began an erratic up and down motion, as if it were trying to communicate something to us that we weren't inclined to see or hear. And we never learned what the light represented, because Mule and I both ran inside, and I cannot tell the reader who outran whom.

We later told the rest of the family about it and had a good laugh. Still later, Mule related the incident to a "jackleg" preacher, who told us that someone was trying to communicate with us from the "spirit world," to tell us that money was buried close by, perhaps in the very spot where we had last seen the light. But neither Mule nor I was ever willing to approach the spot where he and I had last seen the light, so no digging was done.

I began to notice a wistful, faraway longing in Mama's eyes right after Grandma's death. It was as if her death had steered Mama — or a part of her — into another existence, as if something was tugging at her, beckoning for the remainder of Alice to enter into that "other existence" also. It was at this point that Mama began predicting and prophesying her own death, saying, "The sickness I got, no doctor can cure."

The same year that Grandma died, the last of Mama's wayward sons, George, made an unexpected showing. He came and went, but at least he wasn't in prison. This had a very pleasing effect on Mama, for it eased some of the strain I knew she was under.

After George's unexpected showing and departure, Mama's beloved Ruth and her five children (another would come later) came to live with us. She and her husband, Berry, had separated. Her coming was also good medicine for Mama.

In mid-1952, I was ten years old, and growing up pretty fast. Not only was I big for my age, I was also big-minded. During this period, Ruth was a friend indeed, and didn't seem to mind my developing a few grown-up habits — one of them, smoking. Mama had labeled me "mannish," which meant to her that I was trying to be a man before my time. But Ruth didn't object to my doing all the things adolescent boys are supposed to do while growing up. She always made sure that her cigarettes were within reach, so that I could get my quota, which was no more than about three a day.

I remember the day Mama found out that the little girl who had befriended us from Truman Park, and who visited regularly, was really coming so that she and I could get together in the old shed next to the outhouse, and play "games of our own making." At this revelation, Mama was about to drive her knuckles deep into my skull. But Ruth intervened, saying, "Oh shucks, Mama, I don't see why you want to hit him for that. At least we know that he is normal." This stopped me from getting a knuckle drilling from Mama, and it was at this point that I began to see Ruth as a protector to me. Whenever she felt I was being wrongfully accused, she didn't hesitate to intervene on my behalf and oppose anyone, even Mama. This won my love, admiration, respect, and gratitude toward her forever. Ruth's kind nature also won the respect of others with whom she came into contact.

We eventually moved from the house on Wall Boulevard into a bigger and better house. And for a while, we all lived like one big happy family . . .

In 1953, William was sixteen years old. He wanted to enlist in the Army. Being underage, he needed Mama's signature, which she gave. So William, whose ears had provided a substitute nipple for me when I was being weaned from the milk bottle; William, who was my hero after the incident with the rat, and even more so after he saved me from drowning; yes William, who seeing all the other houses on Hendee Street with electricity, decided to put us in the ratings by climbing a pole and running a wire to our house; William, who while we lived on Wall Boulevard, teamed up with a school buddy after school to shine shoes, providing Mama with a few extra dollars; William, who had never touched a cigarette (though nearly five years my senior), who saw one in my mouth at eight years old and kindly slapped it away (and in the process, slapped me as well); William, the quiet, unassuming one, the innovative and resourceful one who — now that I think about it — was never fully a part of us, withdrew the small part of him that was, by enlisting in the Army, and bowed out of our lives for the time being . . .

My great-grandfather's health began to fail sometime after the death of my great-grandmother. Aunt Clem and the rest of his daughters — Mama included — had all agreed that it would be best for him to come to New Orleans so that he could be better cared for. So Grandpa had relocated, and was living in one side of the house owned by Aunt Clem. The last time I saw him, 1954, he had changed a great deal. At eighty-six, Grandpa had lost his burliness and thinned out. His former upright posture was replaced with a stoop. Mama and the rest of his children had all resigned themselves to the inevitable, that he would soon "pass on." As a matter of fact, Grandpa lingered much longer than anyone expected. He knew that Henry, his favorite grandchild, was in prison, and he assured everyone that he would not "pass on to glory" until he saw his grandson out of prison. And so he lingered on . . .

In the latter part of the same year that William went into the Army, to everyone's surprise and pleasure, Henry came home from prison. He had left home when he was fourteen years old; I had no recollection of him. He was now twenty-two years old, and I was going on eleven. I took to him immediately. Henry became the big brother that William had been to me. I admired the way that he established a no-nonsense reputation in the neighborhood, meaning that he was not to be messed with. At the time, I liked the image he projected. And I also loved the fact that, like Ruth, he did not object to me being "mannish" or smoking. In fact, Henry even supplied me with cigarettes.

Not long after Henry came home, he met and married his wife, Emelda, and moved from us. But the big brother image he had established remained with me. At the time, of course, he and I could never be considered peers. But time has a way of closing gaps . . .

True to Grandpa's word, he lived to welcome Henry home. Shortly thereafter, he joined Grandma. Those closest to him took his passing pretty hard. Grandpa was brought back to Gonzales, and his remains are buried in Little Zion Cemetery next to Grandma's.

CHAPTER 8

AFTER WILLIAM'S LEAVING, AND HENRY'S return and eventual departure, I felt there was no one else among my siblings who could take responsibility for me. At eleven, I was the youngest, but I was as big as James, who was going on thirteen. I became my own keeper. I was doing my own thing, carving my own path, and at the same time, trying to mimic the "cool" images the older guys projected. I began trying to play the barrooms, or when I couldn't, the sweetshops — smoking pot, engaging in petty thievery, and just doing whatever appealed to me. I did most of these things, however, under cover. Mama had no idea what I was doing, and I had sense enough to keep it from her.

Mama was known as an excellent cook. She made pastries and such, and she made things taste good. Aunt Clem needed a cook, badly, so she made another showing, appealing to Mama to come over and cook in her restaurant. Mama accepted. Mama would live in one side of a house that Aunt Clem owned, rent-free. At the time, this arrangement suited both Aunt Clem and Mama. This was in 1954, and I was going on thirteen years old.

The area we moved to was mid-city, called "Back-a-town." We lived on Seminole Lane, right off of Jackson Avenue. Aunt Clem's business, which was then a well-known establishment, was called Club Rocky. Her house was better by far than any of the houses we had lived in previously; it boasted six rooms, toilet and bath included. And it had electricity.

I didn't see too much of Mama anymore, for she worked nights and days. Sometimes, however, I would make my way to the club to eat and to see her. The only thorn in my flesh during this period was Aunt Clem's husband, Uncle Willie. I tried to steer clear of him. He was a longshoreman, but sometimes he also worked at the club. When talking about Uncle Willie, family members described him as "having a plate in his head." This meant that most people who knew him thought he was mentally unbalanced. The truth of the matter was, Uncle Willie didn't take no shit from his customers. Years before our moving there, Uncle Willie had shot and killed two allegedly unruly customers. He was never charged for these incidents. In any event, I deliberately avoided him whenever I could.

When we first moved to that neighborhood, James and I could not walk a block without running into other youths who saw our coming as an invasion of their territory, and wanted to "get it on." It was during this time that James and I developed a comradely relationship. Where once we had elected to go our separate ways, we now by mutual consent — and necessity — began hanging out together.

One night, about a month after moving to the neighborhood — and after about six encounters with the local dudes — we decided to take in a movie. Word had gotten out that we had fought with and beaten some of the gang, and that we needed to be "chastised." Unknown to us at the time, our every move was watched. And that night as we neared the corner of South Roman Street and Seminole Lane, about twenty-five figures — ranging from the ages of twelve to seventeen — appeared seemingly out of nowhere and surrounded us. They carried sticks, rocks, bottles, and other indistinguishable objects. The apparent leader of the group came face to face with us, asking, "Y'all got any money?" Almost in unison, we said "yeah." "How much y'all got?" he demanded. And to my surprise — and with all the odds seemingly going against us — I heard James reply, "None of your business."

I looked at James as though he had just tilted the scales of insanity. We had fought many battles, but we had never encountered so many at one time. At the words "none of your business" the leader gave his signal by making the first move. He swung first. And it was definitely on, a free-for-all! Us against them. Once the fight started, I realized that the odds weren't so great after all. In fact, I soon realized that James and I had the advantage, because we had so many targets to choose from, while only giving our opponents two. We received some good blows that night, but we also delivered more than a few. As hard as they tried to bring us down, the harder we fought, refusing to be bested. At times James and I were back to back, and in the gang's eagerness to get us, they only managed to hurt one another. We took their weapons and used them against them. We were making a lot of noise, and a woman's voice yelled, "Y'all cut that out, go on home!" We fought on. A while later, the same voice yelled, "I done called the police!" At the word *police*, individual members of the gang began to fade . . . until there was no one left but James and me. Bruised and a little battered, we headed back home. We never made it to the picture show that night, but we had made a good showing in the neighborhood.

The next day, a gang member who lived across the street invited us over to make friends. That evening, he, James, and I waited in his backyard for the rest of the gang to show up. His house was a regular meeting place for the gang. They eventually showed up, and most wanted to call it square. But some still held grudges. In the end, it was two brothers who held out, who weren't satisfied with our showing and wanted to continue to fight with us. The leader of the gang said okay — but it would have to be a fair, one-on-one fight. James and I gladly obliged the brothers. The fight began in the backyard, but we ended up on Prieur Street, where a large crowd had gathered, grownups and kids alike, to watch the battle. James and I were winning easily, when one of the brothers pulled a hammer from under his shirt. I grabbed his up-raised arm, and the hammer fell to the ground where I quickly retrieved it. I had the hammer raised, ready to strike, when a woman (who I later learned was his mother) ran toward us, pleading, "Please don't hit my child!" Ashamed at what I was about to do, I gave the mother the hammer. In a voice filled with gratitude, she said, "Thank you!" She then grabbed one son by the collar and the other by the arm and dragged them both home.

After that incident, we had no further trouble with that gang. There were other fights, but not with them; they accepted us, and we became a part of them.

When I remember that encounter, I think about the broad lesson that I learned. The lesson was: had we not braved the odds, and stood our ground, we would have become of the doormat of the neighborhood, laid out like a rug for the gang members to walk on. And there was another lesson. People who adhere to (and become blinded by) logic would have told us that we didn't have a ghost of a chance in that battle. But desperation sometimes trumps logic.

Compared to our former home, Aunt Clem's house was a palace, but for all its seeming luxury, it had an artificial ring to it. I never really adjusted to living there. The same feeling of superficiality engulfed me when I attended school. I made good grades, but my desire to learn, to excel, had diminished. I began playing hooky from home and school.

School and home both seemed much too slow and dull, and going to either felt like a visit. I identified wholly with what I had come to believe was the real world: the streets. Summer days, when I should have been in school, were spent at the lake, the beach, or wherever the action was, as long as it wasn't school or home. I expropriated — i.e., shoplifted — small items and converted them into hard cash. And whenever or wherever I could, I expropriated petty cash and converted it into the items I desired. This new path I was cutting was far different from the one I had cut on Thayer Street, a few years earlier. There, on Thayer, I was the mimic, the impersonator. Here, on Seminole Lane, I was the innovator. I soon had my own following: guys who went when I went, came when I came, or who came and went when I said so.

Word finally got back to Mama about some of my unsavory activities. She went behind closed doors with Aunt Clem and Uncle Willie to have a conference about what to do with me. Uncle Willie and Aunt Clem both suggested that I live "uptown," with Clara. Mary, almost 16 now, was also having her problems, and Clem and Willie thought that Mary should also go to live with Clara. But Mary had ideas of her own. Instead of going to live with Clara, she opted to go back to Algiers to live with a friend.

I couldn't (and didn't) make the transition to living with Clara. At the time, there was nothing between us—no physical, mental, or psychological ties whatsoever. So I took it upon myself to depart from Clara after about a week and return home.

Leaving Clara and going back to what I called "home" was a big disappointment. In the short time that I had been gone, things had changed drastically. Mule was rarely seen, and the only people welcomed in that house were Mama, Verna Mae, and James. Anybody else became an intruder. Every time one of them departed, they'd lock the door, keeping me out. Prior to Mama's decree that I live with Clara, whenever I'd wanted to escape from the streets for a while, I always had a place to go for a bite to eat when needed; for a bath, and a change of clothing; or for a few hours of sleep. But now that door was locked. Verna Mae was probably the only one who would have let me into the house, but I couldn't catch her home these days. School was out, and she worked the bar for Aunt Clem. James was loyal to Mama, it seemed, and he wasn't going to go against her decree that I must live with Clara. But once I left Clara's house, I was determined to never go back there, ever, to live with her. All I did now was hang around the streets in my old neighborhood, sometimes with friends, but most times by myself. At night, I would go and crawl under the house that once housed me. I slept with the bugs and the other pests. After about a week of this, unable to bathe or change clothes, even my buddies began rejecting me. James would see me periodically, and he would try and encourage me to go back and live with Clara, but I wouldn't budge. At other times he would offer me food, which I would refuse. After a few weeks of this, James told me that Mama wanted to see me; he also told me that Mama said I didn't have to go live with Clara. I still felt hurt and betrayed, but at this point in my life, I was in no mood to argue with James. He and I had become pretty close, had fought too many battles together, and with these thoughts in mind, I elected to return home with James.

When we reached home, Mama, who was usually at work on these days, was waiting. She came out of her room and gave me a long, curious stare, looking at me as if she were seeing me for the first time in her life. I looked at Mama's face, trying to read something, but couldn't. I did note that she was being extra nice, and this made me wary, put me on guard.

After I'd taken a bath and changed clothes, Mama even gave me some cigarettes. She had never approved of my smoking, so now I *knew* something was wrong. I became very suspicious. I decided to go out and sit on the porch, feeling that if trouble came, it would come from that way. And sure enough, just as I reached the front porch, a late-model car pulled up in front of the house. A well-dressed Black man got out. Instinctively, I knew it was trouble and that it or he had something to do with me. "Is this the Mrs. King residence?" he asked. "Yes, sir," I said. And before the man could ask another question, I went in, passing Mama on her way to the front door to greet the visitor. I stopped in the hallway behind her to listen. Just as I had figured, I was the subject. I heard Mama say to the stranger, "Yes. He is here, and I can't seem to do nothing with him."

I didn't need to hear anything more. I broke into a dead run out the back door. Behind me, I heard James yell, "There he goes!" And there I went, down the ally toward Roman Street, the next street over. There, I met up with a couple of my buddies. "What's going on?" they asked, but before I could answer, I heard the sound of screeching tires. When I looked up, there was the man, with Mama in the back seat of his car, looking for me. I wheeled around and ran back the same way I had come. It was a bit comical, for we repeated this several times. My friends got into the act. Just as I would reach them, they'd shout, "Go back the other way!" and back the other way I'd go. After a while, even the grown-ups in the neighborhood got into the act, yelling, "Run, boy! Don't let 'em catch you."

But I was out of breath, the man was yelling, and Mama was waving her hands in frantic gestures for me to stop. I took one last look up the alleyway, then turned around to face Mama, the man, and the automobile. When the man emerged from the automobile, the first thing he said was: "You must be guilty, innocent people don't run." I wondered, what school did he go to? I knew instinctively that he was from Milny Boys' Home, the juvenile jail in eastern New Orleans. I had passed it many times going out to the lake. Its huge gloomy building loomed like a nightmare. I didn't want any part of it.

But though the man threatened me with Milny, his final assessment was that "all I needed was a good whipping." Mama agreed, but said that I had outgrown her. The juvenile officer — for that's who he was — pointed at Uncle Willie, who had heard the commotion and come to the door, and said, "Well, he ain't outgrown him!" Uncle Willie readily agreed to help Mama chastise me.

I later learned that Mama, wanting to give me a scare, had asked the juvenile authorities to send someone out to "scare me straight." I also learned that Uncle Willie's bite wasn't as vicious as his bark. He didn't do much in the way of chastising me.

So I escaped Milny Boys' Home, and I was back at home with Mama, doing my old routine, and not having to live with Clara. During this period, I was at home a bit more often; I didn't run the streets quite like before.

CHAPTER 9

IN AUGUST 1955 — THREE MONTHS INTO my thirteenth year in existence — Hillary, my biological father, made the scene and I saw him for the first time. Hillary's stepbrother lived not far from us. I had discovered this about two months earlier, and had visited him at his home a few times. He and his wife lived on the corner of Felicity and Rampart streets. Hillary was accustomed to making sporadic visits to the city, and most of the time he would end up at his stepbrother's house, waiting for the effects of his partying to wear off before heading back to Donaldsonville, Louisiana, where he resided. It was on one of Hillary's trips that his brother told him that his son lived nearby.

The day I saw my father for the first time, I was on one of my usual escapades not far from home. One of my friends came running up to me, yelling, "Your daddy is here, your daddy is here!" I must admit, I didn't show much elation or emotion. On the short trip home, I began to think to think about some of those things I had heard from family members: that he had "disowned me"; that I "looked just like him"; and of course that I had his "ways."

When I arrived home, I saw my father for the first time and heard the usual lines a wayward father would say to a child he had all but abandoned. While he talked, I was scrutinizing his every word and taking in his new image and the impression he was projecting. There was indeed a resemblance, and at the time, Hillary's character seemed amiable.

Talk finally got around to the possibility of his taking me back with him to Donaldsonville. Mama consented, saying, "Maybe it's best that you do leave New Orleans, 'cause I fear you gon' get killed if you stay here." In Mama's recent memory was an incident where I was involved in a gang fight resulting in my being stabbed in the back with an ice pick, and nearly paralyzed. But my decision to go to Donaldsonville with my father was not a result of this incident. I consented merely out of curiosity, the urge to explore. That very same day, Hillary and I boarded a Greyhound bus for the ninety-mile trek to Donaldsonville.

Two of the most depressing years of my post-formative period were spent in that town, in Hillary's house. But, I must admit that they were also my best two years. For it was there, in Donaldsonville, that I learned humility, sensitivity, and compassion for the unfortunate. And my thought processes expanded to a capacity much greater than they would have, had I not encountered that experience.

Hillary's house was located on Bryant Street. When we arrived, I was introduced to my "new family" — a stepmother and her two sons (ten and twelve) and a daughter from her previous marriage. Another daughter, Susan, would come later, resulting from her relationship with Hillary. I took an immediate liking to my stepbrothers, and we were almost inseparable. My feelings for my stepmother were mixed. Sometimes I saw her as being kind and sensitive. Most times, I saw her as being akin to the evil stepmother in the Cinderella story. In fact, I recognized the latter before I recognized the former. It surfaced only hours after I'd arrived. Unable to understand the difference between a child growing up in the city and one growing up in the country, my stepmother (who I shall henceforth refer to as Babs) showed her resentment toward me for knowing things she felt I was not supposed to know at my age. But I couldn't do anything about my obvious "over-exposure" to city ways. I responded by resenting both Babs and Hillary. Three days after my arrival, I knew I had hopelessly painted myself into the proverbial corner.

Donaldsonville was (and still is!) a small rural town, with not much to offer by way of excitement. The biggest attraction in those days was the State Fair, which showed up annually and lasted for about two weeks. The majority of the folk in the town, Black and white, would talk about the "coming of the fair" months ahead of time, as if it were the second coming of Christ. There was an old movie theatre that had been abandoned by whites once their new one was built; it was for us. Next door, there was a sweet shop for the Black teenagers. For work, the town boasted a sugar mill, a rice mill, and a sawmill. The rice and sugar mills were seasonal. Most Blacks, and some whites too, had to find work in the surrounding towns.

When I first entered the town, I noticed a large sign bearing the words, "Donaldsonville, the Friendliest Town in the South." It didn't take me very long to learn why this was so. Whites "had their place" and Blacks all "knew theirs." The ones who "knew" their places did the chores for the ones who "had" their places. Other than that, there was no contact — a very good way, I thought, to keep things good and friendly.

The psychology of the townspeople, however, was a trivial matter. What was more depressing was the environment itself, and the restrictions that came with it. I missed the city life to which I had become accustomed. Nevertheless, I convinced myself that I would try to adapt to my new surroundings, and especially to Hillary. I felt that a father-son relationship needed to be established. But my desire to achieve this was shattered less than a week after my arrival. One of my stepbrothers and I were in a discussion, and at some point in the conversation, I made the fatal mistake of saying "Hot dog!" Babs said, "Hillary, did you hear what that boy said?" And without waiting for my father to answer, she explained to him that I had found a "new" way to say "god-damn." He believed her, and his whole countenance changed from one that was friendly, to one of hostility. He then launched an unexpected tirade against me: "You think you're smart just because you lived in the city! If you think you're going to pull that stuff here, you got another thing coming!" I just sat there, shocked and amazed at this rapid turn of events, looking at him as if seeing him for the first time. All the while, I was thinking: "Wow, this isn't the same cat who was so full of smiles to see me a few days ago for the first time in his life." Also, I was wondering how in the world Babs could say that the two phrases were the same, and then convince my father that they were. Maybe my father mistook my confusion for insolence or defiance. At any rate, he then did something I least expected him to do, something Mama had never done: Hillary, the man I had never laid eyes upon until a few days before, walked over to where I stood and gave me a hard slap that reverberated in my ears for several minutes. I was already shocked and amazed at his words, but the way I now felt was beyond description. For this unwarranted slap not only reverberated in my ears, but more so, it reverberated in my heart, and shattered any hopes of my having any affection whatsoever for my father during this crucial period.

That slap was only the beginning. After that first incident, others came in rapid succession.

Not long after that first incident, Hillary — who worked at the sawmill –- asked me to go to the office and get his check. As I was leaving, Babs asked, "What you gon' say when you get there?" I replied, "I am going to tell whoever's in the office that Hillary Wilkerson has sent me to pick up his check." She said, "No! You don't say it like that. You are supposed to say, I come to pick up my father's check, and when they ask you who your father is, then you say, Hillary Wilkerson." And my father, who had been listening, said: "What's wrong, you shame to own me as your daddy?" And following that question came a barrage of threats and verbal assaults that hurt more than a physical beating, or even another slapping, would have had.

Another time, while calculating a grocery bill, Babs asked me to add along with her, to see if we would come up with the same figure. I could see that her sum was incorrect. And for all of my so-called street smarts, I knew nothing about tact, so I blurted out, "That's wrong." Babs replied that she had checked it twice. I still insisted she was off, which was my mistake. For Hillary, who had been watching and listening, said, "What you doin', calling her a liar?" I wisely said, "No, sir, I am not." By this time, I was no longer surprised by my father's irrational rages. And I was never disappointed, for they kept on coming. After that incident, I would watch Babs trying to figure up the grocery bill, and I would wisely keep my mouth shut. Sometimes, she would ask me to check her figures to see if she was right. I would feign adding, then tell her that I had come up with the same figure. She would later learn, however, that we "both" had figured incorrectly. And this would seem to delight her far more than if she had been incorrect by herself.

It was such incidents that caused me to become nervous, mentally uncoordinated, and unsure of myself. For fear of saying the wrong things, I began to be very careful about what I did or didn't say. And as a result of trying to choose the correct response, I began to stutter. My father became infuriated with me, and told me that I had picked up a bad habit, and that I had better stop or he would "whip me until I stopped." And because I couldn't stop right away, I did get whipped. I eventually stopped stuttering, but it was not as a result of his whippings.

In order to keep peace of mind, I tried another approach which should have worked. But, alas, it didn't. I became obsessed with the idea of just remaining quiet, and tried to do so. Both Hillary and Babs would try to make conversation, but unless they directed something at me, I would say nothing. Then Hillary would want to know why I was "wearing a long face." The truth of the matter was, I wasn't angry with either of them; I was just trying to stay out of trouble. But to Hillary, my silent state was insolence, an act of defiance that he wouldn't tolerate. So to appease him, I had to pretend I was happy. As a result, among the other things I had become, I was now "the great pretender" in Hillary's house. But only in his house, mind you. For I had a double that no one could touch . . .

Not long after I arrived in Donaldsonville, school opened and I registered at Lowery High School. This was 1955. School, at this time, was a luxury. For at school, my double surfaced. I was a different person away from Hillary's house. School eliminated some of my depression, and in time I excelled. While I was considered a flop at home, I was a celebrity at school, among classmates and even some of my teachers. Whatever was stripped from me at home, I regained it at school. My confidence, courage, poise, and equilibrium returned at school; while I strove to remain quiet in the presence of my father and step-mother, I was reprimanded by some of my teachers for being too talkative. While Hillary's house was his domain, school was mine. I was selected by my eighth grade classmates to be president of the class. But when school was over for the day, I had to take off my fine dress of confidence and poise, my courage and my stability, and change once again into my usual attire of diffidence and instability, which I was forced to wear at home.

School afforded me the chance to meet a lot of new friends, both female and male. It was at school that I met this girl I'll call Majorie. Each time we'd meet, she would smile at me; I'd smile back. One day, she told me that she wanted to ride home with me on the bus. This meant that she wanted to sit next to me because she liked me. And this was how it started. I eventually grew to like her too. I learned that she lived only a few blocks from me, with her grandmother. Each day when we would get off the school bus, I would walk her home. I wasn't allowed to go into her house because her grandmother was old-fashioned and didn't allow boys to visit her.

Majorie did not dress as well as the other children; most of the clothes she wore were old. As a result, some of the children said that she was "nasty," and later this was changed from just being "nasty" to "doing a lot of nasty things." This gossip didn't stop with the children; grown-ups picked up the chant. People who had never laid eyes on her labeled her as bad. Majorie knew that people were saying a lot of untrue things about her, but she held her head up high, and even tried to be friends with those who she knew talked about her behind her back. She told me that there were only two other boys she had liked, but after they had both tried to make a play on her supposed looseness, the relationships had ended. (Her telling me this made me feel guilty, because I had tried the same thing with other girls.) Anyway, my stepmother learned that I had a new girlfriend, and wanted to meet her. Majorie agreed to come by my house on the following Sunday.

When Sunday arrived, as promised, Majorie showed up and I introduced her to my stepmother. Majorie and I then went out to sit on the porch. After about twenty minutes, Babs called me inside and said, "Boy, what in the world is you doing with that girl? I done heard a lot of bad things about her. Of all the girls to choose from, you had to choose the worst one. I don't think you ought to see her anymore." Eventually, I went back outside to sit on the porch. Majorie, seeing the thoughtful look on my face that had replaced the jovial one I'd had before, wanted to know what was wrong. I said nothing. But I didn't have to. For she had picked up the vibes, and said, "Oh, I see." With those words uttered, Majorie got up and left.

I saw her a number of times at school after that Sunday, but things just weren't the same. But I did feel strongly that I had let Majorie down, the same as the other children and grown-ups had.

It wasn't long afterwards that Majorie's grandmother sent her away to live with a relative — where, I never learned. When she departed, she left me with memories of our holding hands and sharing secrets with each other that we wouldn't dare share with others. Memories of our kissing remained. But that was as far as we ever went . . .

CHAPTER 10

IN DONALDSONVILLE, I LEARNED JUST HOW small the world really was, and that the past is just one step away. Deeds of my past, which I thought I had left behind, caught up with me. One day I arrived home from school, and Babs handed me a letter addressed to me. It was from a company in New Orleans that published a weekly Black newspaper. The letter stated that I owed the company a certain amount of money, and that my failure to pay the company would or could result in their taking legal action . . .

I thought back to the time, in New Orleans, when some of my buddies and I had hustled this company. On Thursdays, the day the paper came out, we would go to one of its many distributors that were located around the city. We would approach the man in charge and tell him we wanted to sell some papers for him. The man would be delighted, and would give us as many as we thought we could sell; sometimes we'd get hundreds. He would take our names and addresses for reference. Once we sold the papers, we were supposed to return with the money and get a percentage. Most times, as planned, we would give the man phony names and addresses, and never return, keeping all the proceeds. But apparently, I had made the mistake of giving him my real name, once. And he had turned my name into the company. The company's representative in Donaldsville was a preacher whose father lived next door to us. This preacher visited with his father on a regular basis and with us on occasions. The good reverend needed someone to sell papers locally, and he offered me the chance to make a few dollars. Naturally I accepted, and even went so far as to tell the reverend that while living in New Orleans, I had once sold papers for that very company. Every Thursday the reverend would bring me a bundle of the papers, and I would walk through the town selling them. And I always sold them all. Four months later, the letter arrived . . .

After reading the letter, I knew I couldn't beat this one, and didn't even try. When Hillary got home and was informed by Babs of the letter's contents, he was furious. But he paid the company the money I owed.

In 1956, for the first time, I had the pleasure of meeting my paternal grandfather, Will Wilkerson. He looked to be in his late sixties. The gap between his and Hillary's age — who was thirty-three years old at that time — was because Hillary was one of his later children. Just how many children Will actually had, I never learned. But I did learn that my grandfather was a "rolling stone," and that "in his day, he was a hell-cat." It was said that many sheriffs of many towns had given him one-way tickets just to get rid of him. I only saw my grandfather twice, and I didn't get a chance to really know him or to hear him tell his side of the story. Not many months after that first visit, I saw Will for the last time, in a coffin. He had died of natural causes.

Sometimes on weekends, after school, I got the chance to hang out with my two stepbrothers. They and their sister lived with their grandmother, but sometimes they stayed overnight with their mother. And during the summer when school was closed, and when Hillary and Babs worked, we would spend a lot of time together. We would "scout" the town and do the forbidden: go swimming in the big muddy Mississippi River, or in the bayous, or the canals. During this time, I would tell them tales of my exploits while I was living in New Orleans, revealing to them things that I wouldn't dare reveal to my father and their mother. They would be fascinated, and come right along with me in thought, as if they were experiencing the same things.

In all fairness, let me say that while there were things that Hillary and Babs did that repelled me and caused my depressive state, they also did things that attracted me to them. For instance, neither objected to my smoking, and they even supplied me with cigarettes. And whenever I couldn't hustle my own ticket money for the "picture show," Babs always made sure that I got it, even when Hillary didn't show up on some Fridays with his paycheck, but would have detoured, spending his time and his money elsewhere. But this seldom happened, and for the most part, Hillary was probably as responsible as he felt he needed to be, or could be. I guess it's true to say that there were whole days when feelings of rejection didn't totally engulf me.

Saturday was movie day, and looking forward to the weekend and going to the movies afforded me the reprieve from depression I needed. But while I liked going to the movies, I was also a lover of music. On my way to the theater, I would have to walk past a couple of juke joints or barrooms, where the jukeboxes belted out the tunes of Big Joe Turner ("Morning Noon And Night") or Little Richard ("Saturday Night"). In tune with music at this point, most times I would walk right past the movie theater, and go next door to the sweet shop, where Chuck Willis would be singing about "The Train That Stole His Love" or Fats Domino would be crying "Ain't That A Shame" — not to mention so many others, such as Chuck Berry, Faye Adams, Bo Diddley, Big Maybelle, and Bobby Mitchell, a product of Algiers. All this was long before the term "rock 'n roll" was coined in Tennessee. Lloyd Price, Ruth Brown, and later, Jackie Wilson and Sam Cooke would emerge as top soul singers. While Jackie may have been "Mr. Excitement" to many, it was the melodious voice of Sam Cooke that excited me and bound me forever to his voice; he simply was my favorite singer. But before Sam Cooke and Jackie Wilson, there were Hank Ballard and the Midnighters, whose "twist" preceded Chubby Checker's by half a dozen years. The dance was considered unacceptable by most American whites, who considered it lewd. In fact, during the early to mid 1950s, many white parents forbade their children to even listen to "Black music." Those young whites brave enough to buy records by Blacks had to hide them, and listen to them while their parents slept or were at work. Until Elvis Presley came along. After Elvis, for some reason, what had once been unacceptable became respectable. It seemed that before White America could accept a Black music creation, or discover the use of the pelvis, they had to see another white perform the feat in public. Elvis was acceptable, and the impact he had on White America was phenomenal; where music was concerned, he brought White America into another dimension entirely.

But before Elvis and his pelvis, Black teens had the sweetshop where we spent our afternoons gyrating to the music of all the artists I have named and so many many more. Those many hours I spent in the sweetshop listening to their music had a consoling affect on me at the time . . .

While my father did many things during this time that prevented any loving relationship that should have developed between a father and son, I did develop a lot of respect for him — until the following incident.

It was late one evening. Besides Hillary, Babs and myself, my two stepbrothers were there to spend the night. We were in the living room, watching television. There was a knock on the front door, and Babs went to answer it. There stood two well-dressed white men, in suits. Without any preamble, one of them asked, "Does Hillary Wilkerson live here?" "Yes," Babs replied. And without asking to enter, both men pushed their way past my stepmother, into the house. I was sitting there, taking all this in, and my first thought was, "These guys are crazy."

I was thinking about Hillary and how he would react. My father was one of those typical Saturday night brawlers. During my year of living with him, I had witnessed first hand on many occasions his fearlessness and brutality towards his peers. Nearly six feet tall, "Red," as most called him, was strong and muscular. I was proud of him, and plenty afraid of him too. But on this night, I had nothing to feel proud about. For after the men pushed inside, they put Hillary through an interrogation that a police officer would envy: *Had he ever lived in New Orleans? Did he ever buy furniture from X's store? Why in the hell had he left without paying the money he owed?* While the men fired questions, Babs was protesting, ready to fight with them and so were we, my two stepbrothers and me. But not Hillary. He acquiesced and became too passive, trying to accommodate them by answering politely.

Finally, one man said, "We want the furniture or the money now!" At this, Babs said, "We paid for those furnitures, now get out of my house!" My two stepbrothers and I joined the act. We began hollering, surrounding the intruders. We made such a fuss that it brought all the neighbors to their doors. I ran to the kitchen, found the biggest knife I could, and returned with it. One intruder asked the other, "You got your rod?" The reply was, "No, I left mine in the car." The first one then said, "Let's get out of here." And they left, but not before promising that they would return. If they ever returned, we had no way of knowing, because not long afterwards, we moved.

When the above incident was happening, I had expected my father to lead the charge. In fact, we all were waiting for this to happen. But it didn't. Not only was I disappointed in Hillary, I was also puzzled. He kept a gun, but he made no attempt to go for it. I felt that Hillary should have made a better showing, but he had performed poorly. And in doing so, he lost more than he ever knew. For not only did he lose some of the respect that I had developed for him, that day he also lost the controlling fear he had over me.

The house we moved to was located on Nolan Avenue. But the change of housing didn't change my status, and I still felt like an outcast. Strangely though — or maybe not so strange — I felt very light-headed and less intimidated by my father and stepmother. The things that they did and said to me did not affect me as much as they had in the past. I was going on fifteen, and I found myself thinking more and more about the folks I had left behind in New Orleans. I felt that there was something I was forgetting or had forgotten. This nudge was persistent.

It was summer 1957, school had closed, and I did my best to get into things that would take me away from home — swimming (by this time they had built a pool for Blacks), baseball, or whatever else I could find to do. One day I mistakenly went off without Babs's consent. It was standard policy that I ask first. When my father came home from work, he learned of my transgression and went into a rage, saying, "I've been watching you lately. You have begun to smell yourself." (Meaning, I was acting like a man.) He went on: "I'm gon' show you just how much man you ain't." He began hitting me. I just stood there, oblivious to the pain, looking at him, unflinching. Our eyes locked, and this time, my look was a deliberate act of defiance. Hillary continued to pound on me harder, but I continued to lock eyes with him, and his efforts to hurt me seemed ridiculous. I think my father finally realized how ridiculous his efforts were. He gave me a look as if he were seeing me for the first time, and abruptly stopped pounding on me. I remained quiet for the rest of the night, deep in thought. I didn't verbally or physically challenge my father that night, but a test of wills had been fought, and I had won. I then made a solemn vow to myself, that never again would I allow my father to abuse me. And it was at this moment that I realized I had finally caught up with my double: we emerged, and together we were one — an entity that Hillary could no longer touch.

Clear-headed and feeling good about myself, I couldn't sleep. A feeling of being refurbished and rested engulfed me. My thoughts began to flow, thinking about the past two years. Then I thought about Mama, and the folks I had left, in New Orleans . . . and then it happened! Something that had been trying to break through for months hit me like a lightning bolt. The thought was like a voice within, which said, "Why don't you just leave, what's holding you here?" I jumped straight up out of the bed. Why, I thought, hadn't I just left? The more I thought about leaving, the more appealing it became, until I was able to taste it. This was like a new secret weapon that I now possessed to be used at my leisure. I would leave, I was sure of that, but when? I knew that I had to leave before school started again. For if I enrolled, the love I had for school wouldn't let me leave Donaldsonville, and I would be stuck for nearly another year. I would leave before school reopened.

Some people will tell you that thoughts are very powerful — that one can *think* something into happening. I don't know if this is true or not, but my secret intense wish was for Hillary to act up again, and to do it quickly. I didn't have long to wait. On this night, as we sat watching television, Babs asked me a question to which I replied with a simple "yes" instead of my usual "yes ma'am." My failure to answer her "properly" on this night wasn't done out of any disrespect, but my father saw it that way. As a result, he lit into me as usual. His verbal attack was intense and abusive. I bore it stoically, glad that it was only verbal. His attack had given me the reason I needed. I knew my next move. I lay awake until about 1:00 a.m., when I knew he and Babs would be asleep. Then, while they slept, and while the town slept, I "tooled up" and crept out of the house. I would need money, I reasoned. I selected a building that was located about nine blocks from where we lived. Using the tool (screwdriver) I had brought with me, I opened a window and entered. Searching the interior of the building, I discovered a small metal box containing about $300. Placing the money inside my shirt, I withdrew from the building and carefully made my way back home. It was now about 3:30 a.m. and the house was still asleep. My adrenaline was making me high, and in this enhanced state, I wanted Hillary to know I had left, and why. So I began to write:

> Dear Daddy (& Babs):
>
> By the time you read this letter, I will be on my way to New Orleans. I don't have to do much explaining as to why I am leaving, because I am sure you already know. In fact, I don't know why the idea to leave hadn't occurred to me a long time ago. Let me say truthfully, that these last two years spent with you were the worst years of my life! I appreciate the shelter, and food, and the little clothing you provided me with these past couple years. And while I cannot repay you for them, I believe I can repay you for the amount

> of kindness the both of you have given me. Here is $50. This will more than cover the amount of kindness you've given me. Sorry I had to leave in this manner, but I didn't want to take the chance of angering you by asking you to send me back or to just let me leave.
>
> Yours Truly,
> *Junior*

I placed the money on top of the letter so they could see it. Day had broken now, and I had to hurry. I changed into the clothes I would bring with me, and with shoes in hand, I eased out the side door, past the window where Hillary slept, then stepped into my shoes and ran all the way to the bus station. When the New Orleans bus pulled out, a sigh of pure pleasure escaped from my throat. And the pleasure I experienced then was the same pleasure I experienced years later, when I escaped from the New Orleans Parish Prison. But that is a story later told . . .

CHAPTER 11

ABOUT TWO HOURS LATER, THE BUS pulled into New Orleans. I learned that Mama had moved back to Algiers, on Magellan Street. I headed straight there. Standing beside James, and having to look down at him, made me realize just how much I had grown. Mama, of course, was still Mama, and had worried about me. During the entire two-year period, I had lost contact with all my relatives who lived in New Orleans. Verna Mae was now married with an infant son, Charles; another son and four daughters would come later. Mary, nearly eighteen now, lived close by with the friend she had taken up with years earlier; Clara, my biological mother, still resided in New Orleans, and Robert, George, and Ruth (with her six children) lived close by. Henry, I learned, was back in prison, at the Louisiana State Penitentiary at Angola; last, but not least, Mule, to my delight, was still around, and still his usual humorous self, still drinking his muscatel. It was like old times only better, among people I felt comfortable with.

About a month after I came home, Houston was released from Michigan State Prison after serving seven years. Everyone was delighted to see him, but for Mama, it was much more than that. For her, it was an ending to an epoch, an answer to a prayer, for she had thought that she would not see him again before her death. Houston was her last object of worry. Henry had returned to prison, but Mama felt that to have lived to see him get out the first time was all that was appointed her. After he went back to prison, Mama spoke of him always in the abstract, with a feeling of detachment, as if she had resigned herself to the fact that she would never again set eyes on him—or, under the circumstances, he on her. I heard her a number of times, saying, "Lordy, I don't want Henry at my funeral with no chains on. If he got to come with 'em on, I don't want him there." This wasn't a prayer, but a statement.

I had been away from Algiers for more than two years. My friends and classmates had undergone a change, just as I had. Some I knew, others I didn't. The girls all seemed to have undergone a beautiful metamorphosis. "Wow," I would say. "What happened to them?"

In 1957, at the age of fifteen, I registered at L.B. Landry High School. I was in the ninth grade. At first, everything seemed to be going okay. My grades were up to par, and I really enjoyed being around my classmates. But eventually, I lost the desire to stay in school. I saw school as a baby-sitter, and I felt I didn't need that. After less than two months, total boredom engulfed me, and despite Mama's desire that I stay in school, I bade farewell to classes and classmates alike . . .

After leaving school, I found odd jobs, nothing permanent. Whenever I couldn't find work, I hung around with older guys, who always talked of "leavin' the south and going north, where things was better." It sounded worth a try to me. So in early November, penniless, I strode away from home, walking with a purpose, with thoughts of going up north, and making scads of money to send back home to Mama. Soon a steady drizzle began, and the temperature dropped. I pressed on, clothes soaked and chilled to the bone. Leaving Orleans Parish meant crossing the Huey P. Long Bridge, but when I neared it, I paused, unsure of myself. There was no law on the books against walking across it. But there was an unwritten law among pedestrians that "one didn't walk across Huey." The risk was just too great. The walkway was pretty narrow, and everyone had heard stories about walkers being "sucked" into traffic.

While I pondered the dangers involved, I saw two dudes — both white, with bedrolls on their backs — heading across the bridge. And I thought, if they can do it, so can I! Remembering

Mule and his stories, I had no doubt that they were hobos. I followed them up the ramp of the bridge. Minutes later, I had caught up with them. My hunch that they were hobos was verified by their smell. The shorter of the two spoke, saying, "By golly, looks like we aren't the only brave ones around here today, huh?" "Yeah, looks that way, doesn't it," I said. I was trying to act casual, as if I had been doing this all my life. At the same time, I was sizing them up. They both looked to be in their mid to late twenties; one was much shorter than the other, who must have been more than six feet tall, and weighed about 250 pounds. Both seemed very friendly. The shorter of the two spoke again: "Ya got a cigarette?" I shook my head, sorry I didn't have one to give him. "Hell, man, ya can't get far without no cigarettes." Reaching into his pocket, he pulled out a sack of tobacco and began rolling one for himself. Afterwards, he passed the sack to me to roll one for myself, which I did. The bigger one asked where I was going. "I don't exactly know," I said, and asked him, "Where y'all headed to?" "Chicago," he said. And as casually as I could, I said, "Well, I may as well go along with y'all, if y'all don't mind." The larger one studied me and asked, "How old are you?" "Eighteen," I said. The shorter one said, "Ya sure are a young lookin' eighteen." "Everybody tells me the same thing," I said. They accepted me as a traveling companion.

We crossed the Huey P. Long Bridge without mishap and we headed for the railroad yard. All the while I was thinking that once I reached Chicago, my worries would be over. I had heard my uncle Houston speak of the city's bright lights and good times. In my reverie, I began hallucinating — I was delirious with the thought of making lots of money, sending it back home to Mama, and later bringing her to Chicago to join me in my new found fame. In this frame of mind, I was impervious to the approaching colder weather and the insistent drizzle of rain that fell. I was brought back to reality when a passenger from a passing car threw a half-smoked cigarette out of his window. "Shorty," my smaller companion, with the agility and precision of an expert, caught the butt before it hit the wet ground. He yelled "a torch!" and began smoking the cigarette as if it had been in his hand all along. I was amazed, and told him so. I also asked him, why "torch?" He told me that in the world of hobos, it was common to collect cigarette butts, it saved them money they didn't have. It was better to find a butt that was already "torched" or lit, for it saved them from having to use their valuable matches. I understood.

We reached the main yard and selected the freight we would ride. We also found cardboard boxes for cushioning and covering. And shortly after 7:00 p.m., the train pulled away. I was tired and hungry and cold. I immediately slept. At about midnight, I awakened with a start, as if someone had poured ice on me: I was freezing. It was at this time that I was brought back to reality. I was ready to abandon my desire for traveling, and would have, too, but after awakening my companions and learning of our location (which was in the state of Mississippi), the urge to jump from the speeding train left me. While Louisiana's legacy of racism and repression of Blacks wasn't much better than Mississippi's, the latter's was more blatant and overt. The memory of the murder of Emmett Till two years earlier was still fresh on my mind. So I decided against jumping off that train. My two companions slept close together, sharing each other's bedding. Thinking about how warm they must be, I couldn't resist the urge to share their covers. So without being invited, I dove feet first into the small gap between them. Shorty said, "Hey Bud', whatcha doin'?" I said, "Shit, I already done it!" Both my companions laughed, and both were soon snoring away. A foul odor emanated from the bedrolls, and from my companions, but I didn't care. I found warmth and comfort in the funkiest place I had thus far ever been.

The train stopped in a small town in Tennessee, where my companions left me, and returned shortly with some crackers and sausage ends. They shared this with me. Other stops we made, we weren't so lucky. Sunday came, and finally the train came to a halt. According to my companions, this place, called "Chinatown," was our final stop in our journey to Chicago. We'd have to hike it the rest of the way. We were all thinking of food, and the long journey ahead of us. We started walking, keeping to the tracks, which would bring us into the Chicago city limits. My bigger companion said, "Look, we got food yesterday, why don't you try your hand at getting some today?" His suggestion was no more than fair, I thought; plus, I was hungry. So with the thought of food dominating my entire being, I headed for the houses in the distance. All of the houses looked alike, and I randomly selected one. I didn't know exactly what I would say, but Mule had told me that a hobo's livelihood depended upon his ability to solicit sympathy and pity from the most callous of individuals.

I knocked on the door I had chosen, and within seconds, a man of oriental descent opened the door. I knew I looked a filthy sight: grease, mixed with grime, covered me entirely. I had also inherited the smell of my two companions. Trembling from the cold, and with a forlorn look in my eyes, I said, "Kind sir, I am so sorry to bother you. But I have been traveling ever since my mother and father died some three years ago, I was twelve years old at the time. I don't have any other relatives, and I am tired of being dirty, hungry, and having no place to go. All I need is a broom. Would you please loan me your broom?" With a perplexed look on his face, the man said, "Why you need broom?" I said, "I just left a nice spot, right off the railroad tracks. It's a little dirty, and I would like to borrow your broom so I could sweep that spot clean. Since it seems like I am going to die, I would like to die in a nice, clean place." I don't know if the man believed me or not, but he opened his door wider, asking me to step inside. He called out to someone — his wife, I suppose — in his native tongue. She entered the room, smiling, and he spoke rapidly in their oriental dialect; then the woman looked at me, still smiling, and bowed and left the room. Moments later, she returned carrying a bag filled with food. She gave it to her husband, who in turn gave it to me, saying, "This much better than broom, huh?" He then laughed out loud. I said, "Sure is." I smiled, thanked them kindly, and bowed out of their lives as quickly as I had entered.

I caught up with my companions. We shared the food (and the story) and continued on our journey. Once we got to Chicago, I thanked them for allowing me to travel with them. We then separated; they going one way, I another.

Before departing from my companions, I had learned from them that the best place to get a meal, and possibly a bed for the night, was at a mission on Madison Avenue. Cold and miserable, I made it to Madison. Hobos lined both sides of the street, trying to find shelter from the frigid winds in doorways, but not having any success. Snow had fallen the night before, and the temperature had dropped into the teens. The mission opened its doors about 8:30 p.m. We all filed in, and after listening for what seemed like hours to a priest or some clergy-related person, we were given "soup" and bread. I ate the bread and gave the so-called soup to another, who gladly gulped it down. Limited bed space sent me back out into the icy winds. After roaming the streets for a while, I found shelter in the bed of a truck. For the next week or so, I slept in abandoned buildings, mostly on the south side. Sometimes I slept in large drainage pipes, using cardboard for covering. During the days, I made my way back to the north side, seeking employment. I had no luck. I also attempted to sell my blood, but since I was in such poor condition, and undernourished, the blood bank would not accept me as a donor.

One morning after leaving one of the employment agencies where jobs were "sold" (which meant that the agency provided daily jobs to a select few for a hefty fee) I met a guy I had seen before trying to get employment. He approached me, saying, "Still no luck, huh, man?" He looked to be about thirty or so, and appeared to be "carrying a stick" (i.e., to be a hobo) like me. I just shrugged. He said, "Look like you could use a meal. Have you tried to sell blood?" "Yeah," I said. He said, "You look kinda young, how old are you?" I gave him the magic number of eighteen. "Where you from?" he asked. "New Orleans," I said. We walked a little further, and he said, "Well, I thought I could help you, but since you say you are eighteen, I won't be able to."

I was curious now, and asked, "How could you help?" He said, "If you were under eighteen, I could bring you to a place where people would see that you got back home." Still wanting to be resolute, I said, "All the help I need is finding a job. Can you help me do that?" The guy (whom I'll call "Buddy") gave me the most incredulous look and said in a loud voice, "Man, you don't need a job! What you need is to get back home to your mama. Anybody can see you don't belong here, and anybody can see you ain't no eighteen, either!"

Buddy went on: "Man, it's like this all over this big raggedy motherfucker! Why do you think there are so many dudes carrying sticks; do you think they *like* carrying sticks? Do you think we *like* doing that?" He continued: "Man, we got pride, we don't like doing this. At one time, I thought I had it made, but now hard times got me, hard times got a lot of us. I am going to git back on my feet, though." He seemed to change gears then, saying, "I don't know what's with you 'bloods' coming all the way from down south thinking y'all gon' come up here and do better. Yeah, a few of y'all gets lucky, but then a few of y'all gets lucky down there, too. So why don't y'all stay down there? All them dudes you saw at them agencies weren't hobos, either. You saw how well dressed some of them was. Them dudes all have families, little children and wives. But they can't find jobs to support them most of the time." He moved me with his rage and frustration, concluding angrily, "Man, there ain't nothin' for the ones who are already here. We all carryin' sticks, we all are just carryin' sticks."

I wasn't ready to give up. I told him I would think about what he said. And I did think about it. And after about three days, with still no luck at finding anyone who would hire me, I ran into Buddy again. I didn't wait for him to ask me. I said, "What was it you said about helping me get back home?"

We ended up at the Traveler's Aid Bureau in the Greyhound bus terminal. We went into the office and the man in charge asked me how old I was. After I told him I was fifteen, he said, "Well, we can get you back home." He introduced himself as

Mr. Collingswoods, the director of the bureau, and asked me a few more questions; then he gave me some meal tickets (which looked like modern-day food stamps) and a sealed envelope and told me to go to the YMCA, where they would be expecting me. About ten minutes later, at the YMCA, Buddy said, "Man, you got it made now. These people will see to it that you get back home." I tried to give him some of the meal tickets, but he refused. We shook hands and said our goodbyes. While I went into the warmth of the YMCA, Buddy headed back the way he had come, into the cold winds of the Chicago streets.

The YMCA was like a hotel. Approaching the guy at the desk, I handed him the envelope and started to explain who I was and why I was there. In a crispy and prissy voice, he said, "You needn't explain. I know all the details." Nevertheless, "Mr. Prissy" opened the envelope and read the letter. Then Mr. Prissy handed me a key with a room number on it. I located the room, saw how neat and clean it was, then located the shower, where I took a long bath, cleaning all the dirt and grime off. Also, I met a brother in the shower who, after learning of my plight, offered me a change of clothing, which I accepted. Afterwards, I went back to my room and slept for more than fifteen hours. When I awakened, it was almost noon. I headed for the cafeteria where I ate a big, luscious meal, then headed back to the Traveler's Aid Bureau. Thinking I would be going back home that day, I hurried my pace. When I got there, Collingswood told me that though he had tried, he could not get in touch with my family. I had given him the right phone number, and I couldn't understand him not being able to contact Mama. He told me to wait while he tried again. He went back into his office and I sat on a nearby bench. After about ten minutes or so, I looked up and saw two policemen approaching. Mr. Collingswood said, "Robert, I still cannot seem to get in touch with your folks. In the meantime, you will have to go with these two gentlemen." My first impulse was to run, but I remained. Angrily, I told him, "Man, if I wanted to go to jail, I didn't need your help, I could have done that on my own." He assured me that it wouldn't be for long.

The officers brought me to a juvenile detention home. The days and then the weeks crawled by. After about three weeks, when I thought I couldn't stand being there any longer, in walked my caseworker. I did what I had seen the others do — I ran over to him and began inquiring about my case, telling him how long I had been there. After thinking a bit, he said, "You should have been gone." He left with the promise of checking it out. About an hour later, he returned and told me that I would be going home that same day — that Mr. Collingswood of Traveler's Aid had insisted on coming to sign me out himself!

A few minutes past 3:00 p.m., Collingswood entered the dayroom, called out my name, and asked, "Ready to go home, Robert?" Was I! I said goodbye to my friends, and we left for the bus station. On the way Collingswood said, "Robert, I am sorry I had to lie to you that day when I told you I had called your people. It was the duty of the juvenile people to do that. After your coming to me, I did the next best thing by calling them and in case of juveniles, this is what I am supposed to do." He went on, "If you had known I was going to call the juvenile people, you would have run, wouldn't you?" I didn't say anything. He had me right.

I was given a bus ticket and five dollars to buy food along the way. Collingswood escorted me to the bus, shook my hand and admonished me to go straight home. And with those words, he departed my world. In time, I would see him (as I saw Shorty and Jim, the couple in Chinatown, and "Buddy") as another signpost along the course of my odyssey.

CHAPTER 12

SITTING ON THE BUS THAT TUESDAY NIGHT, heading back to New Orleans, my mind flashed back over the events of the past month, and I didn't like what I saw. I had arrived in Chicago on a freight train, with the hope of "making it." I was now returning empty-handed on a Greyhound bus, defeated, ashamed, and a little humiliated. Chicago had shown me just how frail and small I was; I had a lot of learning and growing up to do. I was like the frog in the well who jumped out one day and saw that the world was much vaster than he had thought, looking up. Awed and confused, he croaked himself to death. Well, I hadn't croaked myself to death, but I was one hoarse frog.

On the other hand, I rationalized: had not I gained something? In defeat, isn't there also a victory of sorts? Now I knew more about the world outside the South. Before falling asleep, I made a solemn promise to myself. I promised to one day return to Chicago. And this time I vowed it would be different.

To my surprise, no one ridiculed me for my "failure." As a matter of fact I was praised by Mule, Houston, and others, who saw my adventure as something to be proud, and not ashamed, of. That is, all but Mama. She said, "Boy, you ought to be ashamed of yourself. What you trying to do, worry me to death? You leave home, don't tell nobody where you goin', I get a call you way in Chicago. I hope you learnt your lesson."

About three days after returning, I began experiencing excruciating pain in the balls of my feet. They felt as if someone were placing heated irons to them, setting them afire. I couldn't stand or walk without the aid of crutches (which our next door neighbor loaned me when she learned of my predicament) and the only part of my feet that could come into contact with the floor (or anything else) were my heels.

Mama diagnosed my case. She said my feet were frostbitten and brought me to the hospital. After standing in line for what seemed like hours (on my neighbor's crutches), we finally reached the nurse's desk. She bore a sour attitude and had a face to match it. It seemed she had won first prize at a sneering contest and was trying to stay in first place. Or maybe she was a devout member of the Daughters of the American Revolution (DAR). She sneered across her desk, and asked, "What's wrong with you?" This was addressed to Mama, who said, "There ain't nothin' wrong with me. My son has frostbitten feet." I then went on to explain what happened, my trip to Chicago, etc. When I finished, she said, "Well, I am sorry, but the doctors can't do anything for frostbite; there is no cure." After that she dismissed us by saying, "Next person, please," in an exasperated manner. Mama, perhaps not realizing she could have demanded treatment, turned, me following, and left the charity hospital.

Three days later, the pain hadn't yet let up. But I had began to notice that the pain was less intense when I kept my feet away from heat, and from this, an idea took shape: since heat increased the pain, cold would decrease it. I put my idea to test with a tub filled with ice cubes and water. I placed my feet therein and I felt the soothing effects. Wanting to be sure, I pressed the balls of my feet to the tub's bottom. No pain whatsoever. Thinking I had found a cure, I stepped out of the tub and began jumping and shouting. But my joy was short-lived. For after being out of the cold water for about fifteen minutes, my feet went back to their normal temperature, and the red-hot pain was back. Well, so much for the cold water remedy, I thought. But while the ice water didn't make my feet well, it gave me a reprieve from constant pain.

But Mama was determined to make my feet well. She came back one day and said, "Junior, I can't find nothing in the drug store to help you. I talked to the 'drug store man' and told him what you was doing to keep out of pain, and he told me to tell you to stop putting them in that water, if you don't want to lose your feet," I guess

I must have resigned myself to "losing my feet," because I had no intention whatsoever of giving up my "remedy," even if it was temporary.

Unable to find anything at the pharmacy for frostbite, Mama resorted to a cure of her own. She went to the store and bought some rutabaga, which are like big turnips, in bunches. She sliced and dry roasted them, then placed them into thin linen strips and wrapped them around my feet while still scorching hot. She told me that it was an "old folks remedy," and she had no doubt that it would "draw out the frost." My belief in Mama (and her remedy) was the only thing that forced me to endure the intense pain I felt using that method.

I dressed my feet in linen and rutabaga three times daily. The fourth day I was able to stand on them without feeling pain; less than two weeks later, I was walking as good as new.

Ten months had passed since I had returned from Donaldsonville, and I had yet to see my sister, Mary. I had begun to wonder about her. Then one night she knocked on the door. I opened it; she was standing there, holding her abdomen, moaning a little. She asked for Mama, her voice strained. Mama, hearing her name, came into the room and exclaimed, "Child, what in the world is wrong with you?" Mary didn't answer, just continued holding her abdomen. Mama's next words were, "Girl, is you pregnant?" Mary didn't show any signs of pregnancy at all, but Mama was already getting dressed. When she finished, she said, "Come on, Junior, we have to go to the hospital. Mary is experiencing labor pains."

At the hospital, Mary was rushed to the emergency section, Mama with her. I sat in the waiting section. A few hours later I learned that Mary had indeed been pregnant and had given birth to a still-born. The whole process — from the time of Mary's knock upon the door, to her delivery — had taken less than four hours. And on the thirteenth hour, Mary left again, going back to whence she had come . . .

During the early months of 1958, I worked at odd jobs, nothing permanent. Mama worked at odd jobs herself. She had ceased working for Aunt Clem, and had begun working for her other sister, Aunt Alma, who also owned a bar and restaurant. (During this period, the only businesses people of African descent were allowed to run were barber shops, small groceries, funeral parlors, barrooms and churches — the latter three in abundance.) Mama worked part-time for aunt Alma and also did housework for the white lady who owned the grocery store where she had established credit. I had a secret yearning to "retire" Mama from her meager jobs where she earned meager earnings and had nothing to show for her labors but the signs of weariness written on her face and body. But as things turned out, I was left with an unfulfilled yearning for all time . . .

PHOTOGRAPHS

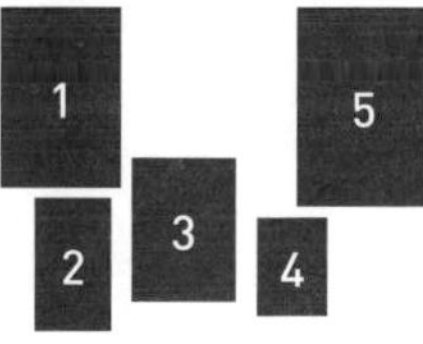

1. My grandmother Alice, who raised me and who I will always call Mama.
2. My sister, Verna Mae.
3. My great-grandmother, Mary Larks.
4. This is my son "Little Robert" who passed away at age five, while I was incarcerated.
5. My uncle, Robert King.

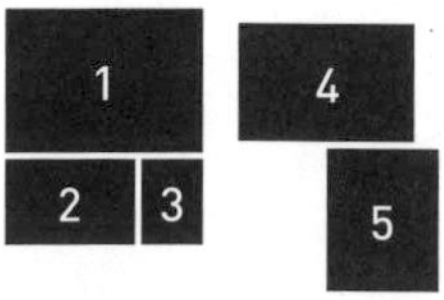

1. Kenya and her sidekick Robert at their new home in Austin, 2008. Photograph by Ann Harkness.
2. Being interviewed in London, 2008. Photograph by André Penteado.
3. Being interviewed soon after being released, 2001.
4. In front of Truth mural by Rigo 23 in San Francisco, declared Robert King Day by Mayor Willie Brown on April 22, 2002. Photograph by Mark Eastman.
5. In front of the "freedom" monument of the African National Congress in South Africa after meeting with the ANC, 2003.

TRUTH

FREEDOM

33 1/3 BOOKS
INTERNATIONAL NEWS MAGAZINES - ZINES - GIFTS
UNCAGE THE PANTHERS
WWW.ANGOLA3.ORG
PRIVATE
PROPERTY

ANGOLA 3
1972
FEBRUARY 8th 2001

ROBERT KING
"BIRD MAN OF BALI"
2004

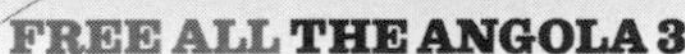

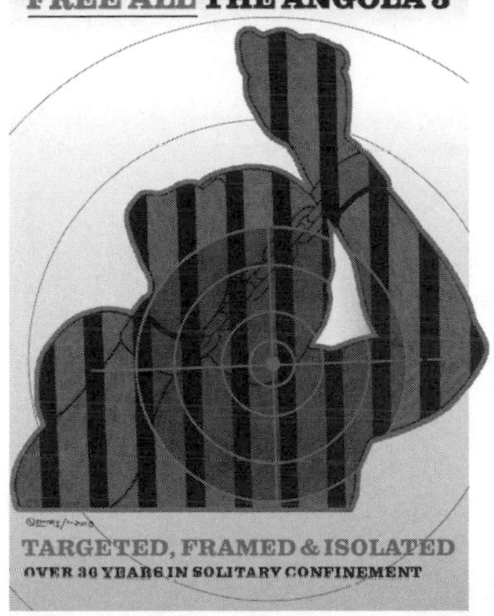

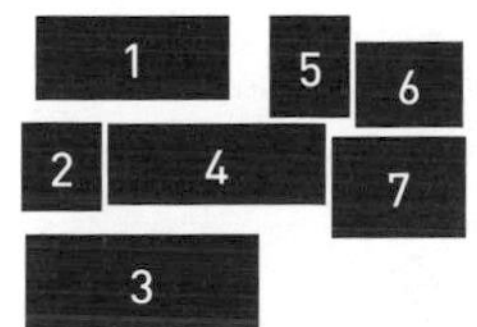

1. Mural by Rigo 23 for the A3 in Los Angeles, circa 2002.
2. Illustration of me by Emory Douglas, circa 1998.
3. Mural by Rigo 23 in Bali painted by local kids upon my visit with Desmond Tutu in 2004.
4. Poster by Rigo 23, done after my release in 2001.
5. Poster by former Black Panther Minister of Culture Emory Douglas to commemorate the Angola 3's 36 years in solitary confinement, 2008.
6. Guards in front of Angola Prison, the "Last Slave Plantation," 2002.
7. Mural by Rigo 23 for the A3 painted by Rigo and scott crow in New Orleans during Critical Resistance, 2003.

FREE HERMAN WALLACE
THE WORLD IS
STOP THE TORTURE
PRISONERS HAVE

FREE THE ANGOLA 4
FREE THE ANGOLA 4

LOUISIANA STATE PENITENTIARY

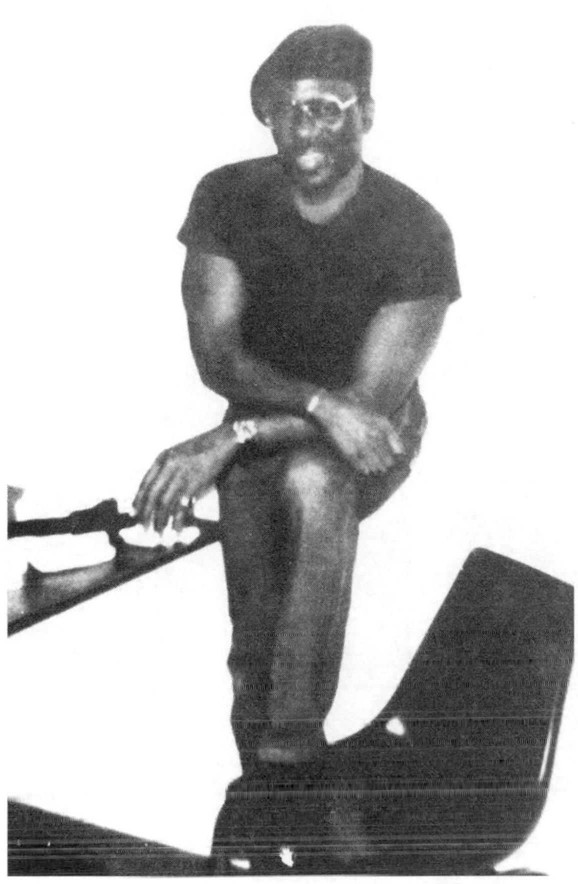

1 | 2 | 3 | 4 | 5

1. First protest against solitary confinement in front of Angola prison, and my first time to return to the prison since my release, 2002.
2. Protest in support for the original "Angola 4" (before the original cases were dropped). In the foreground is Jill Schaefer, a known FBI COINTELPRO informant, who disrupted and stole money from the original support committee, c. 1973.
3. Protesting Herman and Albert's confinement in front of Angola, 2002.
4. Herman Wallace in the 1970s.
5. Albert Woodfox in the 1970s.

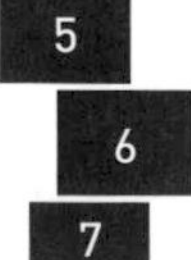

1. Making Freelines candy at my home in Austin after Hurricane Katrina. Photograph by Ann Harkness.
2. Elatedly walking out of Angola Prison after 31 years, 29 of them spent in solitary confinement, February 2001. Photograph by Marina Drummer.
3. The only picture of the Angola 3 together, from left to right: Herman Wallace, Robert King, Albert Woodfox, 1990s.
4. Herman Wallace and Albert Woodfox during rare visit, and their first time to see each other since the early 1990s, c 2001.
5. Meeting my uncle William as adults after my release in 2001.
6. With former U.S. House Representative Cynthia McKinney, 2007.
7. With my good friend, and former Black Panther Minister of Defense Geronimo Ji Jaga (Pratt) who also served 27 years as a political prisoner before being released, 2007. Photograph by Marina Drummer.

1
2 3
4

1. Me with kids in Pretoria, South Africa, 2003.
2. From left to right: Lawyer Denise LaBouef, The Body Shop co-founder and head of the Roddick Foundation Gordon Roddick, and me in New Orleans 2008.
3. Greeting supporters at my release from prison, former Panther Marion Brown on left, February 2001. Photograph by Marina Drummer.
4. From left to right: Joju Cleaver (daughter of Former Panthers Kathleen and Eldridge Cleaver), me, U.S. House Representative Maxine Waters, Former Panther Geronimo Ji Jaga in New Orleans, 2005.

1. King with Gordon Roddick (left) and producer Vadim Jean (right) in London at viewing of *Land of the Free*.
2. King speaking at TED in San Francisco.
3. Poster promoting documentary, *Land of the Free*.
4. King and Geronimo (left).

1. Protest at front gate at Louisiana State Penitentiary with Herman Wallace's sister, Vicki Wallace (far left), Jackie Sumell (left), Brackin Firecracker, and King.

2. King with (from left to right) Dean John Welch, Gina Brown, and Valerie Palm in Pittsburgh.

1

2

1. King in New Orleans points at billboard depicting the 39th commemoration of solitary confinement.
2. Supporters at hearing for Herman Wallace at courthouse in Baton Rouge, LA,in 2003.

1

2

1. Supporters commemorate 40 years of solitary confinement in April 2012 at state capitol in Baton Rouge, LA.
2. Mada McDonald pictured right of King, Woodfox's brother, Michael Mable (far right), and Wallace's sister, Vicki Wallace (right of Mada).

1

2

1. Supporters commemorate 40 years of solitary confinement in April 2012 at state capitol in Baton Rouge, LA.
2. Family and friends show support at "40 Years of Solitary Confinement" commemoration. Back row, left to right: Brackin, Jack, Nata, King, Everett, Vicki, Michael, and Angela. Pictured in front: Mwalimu.

1

2

1. At "40 Years of Solitary Confinement" commemoration.
2. King speaks to Baton Rouge media at "40 Years of Solitary Confinement" commemoration.

1

2

1. King addresses supporters at "40 Years of Solitary Confinement" commemoration.
2. Photo of Amnesty International folders containing nearly 70,000 signatures worldwide petitioning Governor Jindal to release Herman and Albert from solitary confinement.

1. King with Rigo 23 [middle] and Geronimo [right] in Morgan City, Louisiana, 2003.
2. King in Austin, 2006.

CHAPTER 13.

UP UNTIL 1958, MANY MEMORABLE EVENTS (some wanted, others unwanted) had transpired during my short life span. But that year ushered in an event that will follow me to my grave . . .

The day began like any other summer day, bright and sunny, lively and vibrant, a day easily taken for granted at fifteen. Walking with a friend, having nothing to do and not having seen Ruth lately, I decided to pay her a visit. We were met at the door by her eldest daughter, Ida, who was eleven at the time. She said, "Junior, she's sick." "What's wrong with her?" I asked, entering the house. "I don't know, just sick," said Ida. I went straight to the room where Ruth lay on a bed, under a large pile of blankets. I found this strange because it was a burner outside, and much hotter inside the house. Concerned now, I asked, "What's the matter, Ruth?" When she heard my voice she opened her eyes and said, "Oh Junior, I didn't know you were here. I have a little fever, that's all. I'll be alright." Looking down at her and seeing the beads of sweat upon her forehead, I asked, "Do you want me to go and get Mama?" knowing I would do so anyway, even if she said no. But she said, "Yes, go and get her, I want her to go to the hospital with me." I made haste to get Mama, who, upon hearing that her "best child" was ill, dressed quickly, went to Ruth's house, and from there they both went to the hospital. This was at about 1:00 p.m.

Six . . . seven . . . eight o'clock, and neither Mama nor Ruth had made it back. I went to bed early that night. About 9:00 p.m., I heard the insistent ring of our neighbor's phone, then her knock on the wall (signifying that the call was for someone on our side of the house). "James, it's your Mama," I heard her say before dozing off again. The next I knew, I was being shaken violently by James. I remember saying, "Man, let me sleep." But his insistent shaking kept me from going back to sleep. "Wake up, Junior! Ruth is dead . . . she's dead."

No, no, no, I thought; I'll wait until Mama comes home and she'll tell me better. Maybe the doctors had made a mistake. Maybe the phone will ring again, and Ruth will be alright . . . I actually willed myself into some kind of suspended animation, which lasted until Mama came home a few hours later and told us again that Ruth had died.

I tried and tried and tried to will it not to be. No. Not her, not Ruth. Not the understanding, the compassionate one. My Defender, my personal angel, protecting me from those who would harm me. Dead at the age of thirty-two, an untimely death.

Once the event had passed, I was able to piece together the circumstances which led to her death. After she and her husband, Berry, separated, Ruth had applied for and got on welfare with the stipulation that she couldn't have any more children. Her social worker had rubbed it on thick, had told her that if she came up pregnant, they wouldn't hesitate to cut her off. Ruth held firm for four years, then became pregnant. And it was this pregnancy that cost her her life.

Verna Mae, also separated from her husband, lived with Ruth. She was the only person besides Ruth who knew about the pregnancy. They had talked about it and decided to keep it from Mama and the rest of the family. Ruth knew she had to get rid of the baby, as Verna put it, but she kept putting it off. When she did decide to go through with it, she was more than four months pregnant. Whatever it was she took, it not only destroyed the life growing within her, but herself as well. Whatever the substance was, as Mama put it, "it ate up her insides" and proved fatal. I've known a few major hurts in my lifetime. The death of Ruth was my first and foremost.

When it came to grieving over Ruth's demise, I wasn't alone; everyone in the family felt it, but Mama more so. During the wake and the funeral, raw, naked grief poured from her. One could almost reach out and touch that grief. She would repeat over and over, "Lord, I wanted Ruth to bury me; I wanted her to bury me."

With Ruth gone, her six children came to live with us. Besides Ida Mae, there were Clarence, Doris, Larry, Shirley, and Charles. Mama wanted to keep them all together. She had always maintained that it was unhealthy for a family to be split apart. I felt real close to Ruth's children and was glad that they were with us. But this arrangement was not destined to last very long, for while Ruth's children would remain together and eventually grow up together, it would not be with us . . .

About five months after Ruth's passing, Mama allowed herself to be taken to the hospital. I say "allowed" because she put it off as long as she could. Mama knew she was sick and knew that this sickness was unto death. The day she went to the hospital, we learned that she had cancer and the doctors had given her no more than six months to live. This was September 1958.

Mama was in the hospital about two weeks before coming home. Thereafter, it was back and forth to the hospital for a few months, and finally she was sent home to die. Aunt Carrie, Mama's eldest sister, who had nursing experience, came from California to "make y'all Mama comfortable before she die." And in the process, she never ceased to remind us that it was worrying about us that had caused Mama to want to die. "Y'all Mama knew she had cancer, but she wanted to die. Y'all wore her out. She deliberately waited until it got to the stage it was, to make sure the doctors couldn't cure her." If Aunt Carrie was trying to make us feel guilty, she sure enough succeeded where I was concerned.

During this period, I felt closer to Mama than I ever had before. The only time I would leave the house was when I managed to find a little work, which was seldom. I wasn't the only one who had begun to realize that Mama would be lost forever to them. Everyone else realized this too, especially Mule. The only word that can describe Mule during this time is subdued. Mule, always quick-witted, could not find any retort to the voice of death.

As time passed, Mama's condition worsened. Aunt Carrie wired William, who was in the Coast Guard, stationed in Maine, telling him that Mama didn't have more than a week or so left. A few days later, William was home with a week's leave. Prior to his coming, Mama had been having "ups and downs," but while William was home, she seemed to be more up. I believe William soon got the idea that Aunt Carrie and the doctors had been wrong. I know I did. To my delight, Mama looked to be on the road to recovery. When the week was up, William headed back to base. Before he left, Aunt Carrie said, "I wish you had gotten your leave extended, 'cause you gon' have to come right back." She was right.

A day after William left, Mama's condition "dropped pretty low," as Aunt Carrie put it. She told us to stay close, because Mama would die that night or no later than the following day.

The next day Aunt Carrie called all of us who were at home into Mama's room and told us, "Y'all Mama is dying." I stood at the foot of the bed, looking down at the now-withered form of Mama. The pillow on which she rested her head seemed to engulf her and made her seem smaller than she actually was. There was a struggle for breath; I moved closer to the bed. Her breathing resumed, but was irregular. An intake of air . . . a pause . . . an expulsion. Inhale. Pause. Exhale. The time between her breaths became longer . . . finally I watched the last shallow intake of breath . . . and the final sigh. Mama, having birthed nine children and raised two more (my sister and me) "gave up the ghost" at the young age of forty-nine. Aunt Carrie, now crying along with everyone else, said, "There goes Monk; there goes y'all Mama." This was March 1959.

Ruth's death had caught me unprepared and the impact it had had on me had sort of used me up. Mama's death did not have the same impact; it was expected, and we all had gotten used to the idea. But while the two deaths didn't have the same impact on me, they bore the same significance; I had lost two champions, two giants.

At the funeral, all of Mama's children, except Henry, were there. William had returned from Maine. Mama was eulogized in the church she had joined after leaving Gonzales, St. Stephen's Baptist Church. Then we all piled into automobiles and made the trek back to Gonzales, where a brief service was held for her in Zion Baptist Church, the church of her youth. Afterwards, Mama was laid to rest next to Grandma and Grandpa.

After the funeral, family members and friends went their separate ways, never to be seen again. Among those was my uncle, William. After the funeral, he went back to the state of Maine. A few years later, he and his wife, Evelina, and their children moved to Oakland, California. From the day of Mama's funeral, up to the time of this writing, none of the family (except James, for a brief period) he left behind, had seen him. So indeed, William, the quiet, thoughtful, resourceful one — who in hindsight never seemed a part of us left our lives for many years to come.

Less than a month after Mama's death, all of Ruth's children went to live with a paternal aunt, where they all grew up together, fulfilling Mama's wish.

CHAPTER 14

APPROACHING MY SIXTEENTH BIRTHDAY, less than two months after Mama's death, I was walking with two companions, Calvin and John, when we were unceremoniously stopped and arrested by police, who said that Calvin and I fit the descriptions of two men who had robbed a gas station two weeks earlier. At the station, under pressure, John told the cops that he didn't know whether Calvin and I had robbed the gas station or not, but that we had talked of robbing places and had asked him if he knew of any good places to rob. This strengthened their suspicions against the two of us. So what began as a routine investigation turned out to be a case against Calvin and me. We were charged with the robbery.

Calvin, approaching twenty, would be tried as an adult if he went to trial. Instead, he copped out for five years and was sentenced to Louisiana State Penitentiary, at Angola, and later transferred to the state's only youth prison, DeQuincy. I went before a juvenile court. The judge, whose name was Blessing, decided to bestow a blessing upon me by sentencing me to an indefinite stay at the state reformatory in Scotlandville, called "Scotland" by most people. It was said that when Judge Blessing was deciding your punishment, he would fold his hands in front of his stomach. If he twirled his thumbs in a forward motion, it meant you weren't going to Scotland. If he twirled his thumbs in a backward motion, you were going to Scotland for sure. I watched intently and knew where I was heading before he told me.

The thought of going to Scotland (whose proper name at the time was State Industrial School for Colored Youth) didn't disturb me one bit. So much bad had happened to me in so short a period of time, I felt that nothing could be worse than what I had already encountered. I nevertheless wondered what it would be like.

The trip from New Orleans lasted only a few hours. At a little before noon, the car pulled up at the front gate of the place that would be my home for the next year. At first glance, I thought the driver had made a mistake and that we had pulled into a college campus. But a dude who had run away and was being brought back with me, assured me that it was the reformatory.

I was brought to an office in the administration building and told that I would be residing in one of the "big boys'" dormitories. On the way to the assigned dormitory, the "runner" (an inmate whose job it was to escort new arrivals) brought me to a small house resembling a shed. A man sat by the door, and from his vantage point he could see the entire campus. The runner said, "Got one for you, Reverend Pert." In a deep voice that sounded like thunder, the Reverend said, "You heard what the runner called me, didn't ya? But just in case you didn't, I am going to repeat it. My name is Reverend Pert, and like everyone else here, you'll call me that." By now he had stood up. And I noticed just how much bigger he was than me. Continuing, he said, "You from N'aw'leans. I hear y'all likes to gang fight. Well, we don't 'low no gang fights here. You either go to school or you work. On Saturday mornings you are 'lowed to play on campus 'til noon. Afterwards, you watch television, and some Saturdays, you get a chance to dance." I was a little confused at his saying I'd get a chance to dance, but I held my tongue. The Reverend went on: "Sunday you go to church. If you got any money in your account, you can draw two packs of cigarettes and a quarter every week. You will be living in Pinecrest dormitory, and you will line up over there." I thought he had dismissed me, but the Reverend had one other admonition. "Oh, yes, one last thing. While you are in the dining hall, dancing or whatever, there will be no feelin' on the girls." I was more confused than ever. Of all the talk I had heard about Scotlandville, I had never heard that there were females housed there.

After being dismissed, I strode into the midst of a group of boys hanging out and playing games. Not many minutes later, I heard something that sounded like a bullhorn. It was Reverend Pert, bellowing long and loud. His bellow carried from one end of the campus to the other, and brought an immediate end to all activities. I saw dudes lining up in all directions, in front of their respective dormitories. After being counted by the "housefathers," (the men supervising the dormitories), we headed for the dining hall.

Being a new boy, and not having changed from my street clothes into standard issue khaki shirt and pants, I stood out like a tin can in a pile of bottles. As I entered the dining hall, I heard "a new boy" and "bet he's from the Crescent City." It was not so much what was being said as who was saying it that caught my attention. Girls! Long tables filled with some of the most attractive girls I'd ever seen; they were beautiful, and they were bold. Some even reached out to grab my hand, despite the admonishing they got from their housemothers (female supervisors). I didn't say anything, I only smiled and looked and took pleasure in the sight.

That first day, I made a lot of new friends. As a matter of fact, every brother who was from New Orleans was "my friend." The reasoning behind this was that there were inmates from nearly every part of Louisiana: New Orleans, Shreveport, Baton Rouge, Monroe, Lake Charles, Lafayette, and other unheard-of places. In spite of Reverend Pert's rules, gang fights were the order of the day, and your hometown determined both your friends and your enemies.

I had a choice of going to school or work. I elected to go to school. About two weeks later, I was leaving one of my classrooms for a recess period when this sister I knew from the streets, Louise, came up to me and said, "Robert, do you know Cat?" The answer was no. Louise went on: "Well, she told me to tell you that she digs you, and that she will be standing at the far end of the hallway at break. If you want to see her, you can meet here there." I was about to go to the restroom and sneak a smoke, but I detoured back the other way. Louise had waited for me to decide and walked with me. As we neared the end of the hallway, she pointed to one of the most beautiful girls I had ever laid eyes on and asked, "Well, do you dig her?" And I almost screamed: "Yes!"

Cat and I got acquainted that day and I fell in love with her. Cat was a beautiful, charcoal-black sister who could be picked out in a crowd of a thousand. Just looking at her, one had to wonder how a girl like her could have ever ended up in a reformatory. Cat and I sat at the same table, wrote love letters to each other, to be read at night, and promised that we would marry as soon as we were released.

A few days after meeting Cat, I noticed this brother watching me; he had a mean, vicious look on his face. They called him Pugnose because of his alleged boxing ability. He wasn't one of my enemies, because he was from New Orleans, so I wondered just why he was "eye-fighting" me. I soon found out. He told everyone in the dormitory that I was messing with his girl, and that he "had a cake baked for me." He and Cat had actually broken up, but that didn't make any difference nor did it make any difference that Cat had chosen me. I was told by some of the guys that my going with Cat was going against the code, breaking a long-standing rule which held that once a courtship existed between a boy and a girl, even though it had ended, the girl could not court any other boy as long as the first boy remained in the institution. The boy could court another girl, but the girl still couldn't court another boy. This didn't make any sense to me, and code or no code, I decided that I would continue to court Cat for as long as she wanted, and Pugnose could continue to stare, glare, and snare if he wanted to. I didn't care. I could have taken the low road and tried to reason with him, tried to convince him that the code was unfair. But that wouldn't have done any good. After telling everyone that he had a cake baked for me, he had to make good on his euphemistic threat. Too, I was new on the set, and there was no way he could let a new guy break the code, especially at his expense. He would have looked like a chump.

Fighting was, of course, taboo, and anyone caught doing so faced the supervisor's paddle or strap. But boxing was a sport. Every afternoon, during school days — weather permitting — we had a recreation period. On this day, the teacher/coach held a pair of boxing gloves high above his head and said, "Alright, who wants 'em?" Pugnose quickly reached for a pair and began putting them on. No one else moved. The teacher said, "All right, who wants the other ones?" Still no one moved. By now everyone knew the tension between Pug and me, and everyone — even the coach — had their eyes focused on me. I heard someone said, "He wants you, Robert, go ahead!" I still didn't move. Pug, now much more sure of himself, reached over and grabbed the gloves from the coach's hand. Then he handed them to me. While I put the gloves on, Pug went into his stance; shadow-boxing and beating up on the wind.

In case the reader has been wondering, the truth of the matter is, I wasn't afraid of Pugnose, despite his reputation as a boxer and a brawler. By this time, I had fought many street fights, and while I hadn't yet learned "scientific boxing," I instinctively had the art of fighting down pat. After lacing up the gloves, I squared off with Pug and he and I began to swap leather. I think I surprised everyone, especially Pug. He was just a routine slugger, and his mechanized, predictable moves were no match for my undisciplined street style. I threw punches from every possible angle, and connected most of them. To sum it up, Pug didn't have a chance that day. After the fight, he was admitted to the infirmary for three days. When he returned to the dormitory, he kindly gave me his blessing to continue my relationship with Cat. The code was broken. We became sort of friends.

Not long afterwards, Cat went home to New Orleans and from there, her mother sent her off to Connecticut to live with a relative. She and I communicated for a while, but as with all fires, when there is no feeding of the flame, it eventually dies out. Maybe it just wasn't our time.

As a result of that incident with Pug, my status on the campus rose, both among the inmates and the supervisors, especially the coaches and teachers. I did well in school, and I played every sport well, except basketball. I soon learned that once a status was achieved, it decreased one's chances of coming into contact with the supervisors' straps, which were used unsparingly at the time. I worked in the kitchen when I wasn't in school. The cooks, mostly women, went to Reverend Pert and told him, "Reverend, that man (I had convinced them that I was nineteen years old) is gittin' outta hand, and you gotta do somethin' 'bout him." Reverend Pert came to me and told me that since they had complained, he had to "satisfy the wimmin folks." He gave me a few token swats with the strap, telling me, "You understand, I got to please the wimmin folks." I understood . . .

During the Christmas holidays, the reformatory had a policy to allow some of the inmates a visit home. I was granted a five-day leave.

Verna Mae now lived in the house on Magellan Street where Mama used to live. When I got home, Verna Mae was there, and so was her friend, Cherry. Cherry and I got acquainted and made passionate love throughout the night. Prior to Cherry, I had never had intercourse with a girl. (I don't count the girls I used to "play house" with before reaching puberty.) Cherry was the same age I was, approaching seventeen, and we spent the nights in heaven, at least for a while. Then all hell broke loose. For Cherry, I learned, had no "cherry." She had had multiple partners before me, and one of them had given her a venereal disease, which she in turn had passed on to me. When I returned to the reformatory, the head of my penis had swollen to twice its normal size, and a foul odor emitted from it: it dripped, and hurt like hell. I had what some termed "the bull-head clap." A better word was gonorrhea.

I was expelled from the State Industrial School for Colored Youth in 1960. As I was leaving, my counselor said, "Well,

Robert, you know you can't come back here. Your next stop is the penitentiary." He said this as if he knew or understood the inevitable link that existed between the colonized subject and prison: that Black men reaching a certain age were — as George Jackson put it — destined for prison or the grave . . .

CHAPTER 15

VERNA NOW LIVED ALONE IN THE HOUSE that Mama used to occupy. After Mama's death, Mule had moved out; also James, who, after a short stay in Maine with William, now lived in Chicago. Houston, Robert, and George lived nearby and visited occasionally. When I got home, there was no welcoming home party in the traditional sense. Verna Mae was there to greet me, and with her was Ellen.

I had known Ellen for years. She was about five years my senior. Her younger brother, Clifford, and I were friends. Looking at Ellen that day was like seeing her for the first time. She and I got reacquainted, and intimate, that day. I didn't have any real sense of what a relationship between a man and a woman meant, until Ellen. She taught me the ropes about sex. She led and I followed. I caught on quickly, and in time we became equals.

I now had responsibilities to shoulder, and a job was essential. For the first months after leaving the reform school, I managed to find temporary employment. During this period, Louisiana (or maybe it was just New Orleans) had a "vagrant law" which required males of working age to show "visible means of support." Policemen could stop a male (especially a Black male) and ask for check stubs, employer's phone number, etc. If he couldn't show sufficient "means of support," the police had the power to arrest him, and hold him in detention for seventy-two hours; the law became known as "The 72." The cops had a field day abusing this law, applying it to Blacks even when support was evident. The few times I was arrested on a "72," I produced check stubs proving I worked. Nevertheless, I was charged, booked, and held for 72 hours under "investigation." I would get arrested on a Saturday night and be held until Tuesday night. When I returned to work, someone else had usually taken my place. But I was lucky. Many brothers who were arrested on a "72" ended up doing time in prison. While being investigated and interrogated, they would be coerced by the police into signing "confessions" to unsolved crimes.

Not long after my release, I learned that Hillary, my father, had moved back to New Orleans. Babs had also returned to the city, but she and my father — while seeing one another on occasions — were separated. I met with my father. Even though I had "hated" him and Babs during my adolescent years, I concluded that nearly all children when growing up at some point "hate" their parents. I was no exception. As it turned out, Hillary and I had a good reunion; he recognized me as an equal and, in time, we developed a pretty good relationship, considering all that had happened.

The inability to find secure employment and matching pay, pushed me beyond the tolerance level; my desperation launched me into a direction contrary to the acceptable modes of society. I became a petty thief. I thought I was being discreet, and I was not violent in my acts. However, despite what I considered my discretion, by early 1961, I was being pursued in earnest by the New Orleans police for "questioning." I had become a fugitive in my own hometown. So with the cops on my heel, I left the state and went back to Chicago.

As I alluded to earlier, James, after a brief stay in Maine where our brother William was stationed, had moved to Chicago. After a week or so of wandering about the city of Chicago, I found James on the South Side. He managed to get me a job where he worked, and while in Chicago this time, I really got a chance to see what the glamour was all about. It was a huge city, teeming with all kinds of activities. I got the chance to patronize the famous Club Delsia, which was frequented by all the big names of the time. I also got the opportunity to visit the infamous "47th and Calumet" area, where women of all shades and races, all types and ages, advertised their wares: "Hey Daddy, you want a date?" and, "Honey, come my way, she can't do anything for you, I can." The lines of women in competition extended for blocks. Their pimps, not far away, gambled in the hallways, competing with one another as ardently as their whores did for tricks. This was Chicago; this was part of the "bright lights."

After about five months of Chicago, I became restless, moody, and homesick, and perhaps a little lovesick for Ellen, too. Loving and missing Ellen had the effect of dimming my vision of what awaited me should I return to New Orleans. But James, sensing my mood, and having no real knowledge of my extra-curricular activities back home, suggested that I take a short leave of absence, which my job allowed. This was all the urging I needed. I made arrangements, boarded a bus, and headed back to New Orleans and disaster.

About ten days after being back from Chicago, I teamed up with a couple of my "Scotlandville" buddies. We met at the lake that day — picking up two more buddies — and decided against swimming in favor of riding around in an old jalopy belonging to one of them. Early that evening, while driving around in the downtown area, we were converged on by police cars, flashing their lights, sirens wailing. Policemen with drawn guns ordered us out of the car. According to them, three of the men in our car (there were five of us) fit the description of three men who had pulled a couple of robberies earlier. Upon seeing one of the cops, my heart sank. For he was the cop everyone called "Minnie Cat," the same cop who had been responsible for my going to the reformatory. He now headed the arrests and the subsequent investigation.

As it turned out, none of the alleged victims identified me as being a perpetrator of either of the robberies. Steve, Duck, and Jellybean, however, were tentatively identified as being participants in at least one, if not both, of the robberies. It was assumed by the officers that since I wasn't identified, I must have been the driver of the getaway car. On this theory, I was booked. This theory could have been easily disproven had I been able to afford an attorney, because at the time, I didn't know beans about driving an automobile and couldn't tell the difference between first gear and neutral. A paid attorney might have been able to get this fact across even to an eager prosecutor who couldn't care less how a conviction was obtained. But as it turned out, the theory that I had driven the car persisted, and in the end, prevailed.

The other, lesser crimes I was supposedly wanted for before leaving for Chicago paled in favor of this new and bigger crime. After a brief stay in one of the city jails (called precincts at the time), we were shipped to the New Orleans Parish Prison to await the outcome. Lawyers appointed by the state approached us, mostly to get us to plead guilty, or "cop-out" for the ten years that the district attorney was offering. This ten-year offer was made to everyone except Jellybean, who, having no juvenile record, was offered seven and a half years, which he promptly accepted. The rest of us held out — for a while, anyway.

In 1961, the maximum sentence for an armed robbery was thirty years. Since then (and at present), it has more than tripled to ninety-nine years. And if one is unlucky enough to have a prior conviction, a 198-year sentence is common. But there we were with our lawyers telling us we didn't have a chance of "beating the rap"; with the district attorney threatening to give us the whole thirty years if we went to trial; and with jailhouse lawyers urging us to cop-out and "run with the ten years," or we might end up like Cocky Lindy (the nickname of the brother who was the first to receive the thirty year sentence, after refusing to cop-out). With pressure coming from all sides, the three of us — Steve, Duck, and I — talked it over and decided to "run with the ten years."

The promotion from a juvenile facility to an adult prison didn't take long, and it was quite easy: all it took was for me to plead guilty to an alleged armed robbery that two people committed but four pled guilty to.

CHAPTER 16

ANGOLA PRISON WAS KNOWN BY A NUMBER of aliases at the time: the Bottom; the River; the Ponderosa; the Mound; the Farm; the Hill — and probably many more which have escaped through time. Its location, then and now, is in the backwoods of northwest Louisiana.

After traveling north on Highway 61 for a couple of hours, just before reaching the outskirts of St. Francisville, the police van turned off onto a stretch of narrow, winding road flanked on both sides by dense woods. Every now and then, a house came into view, as if to remind us that this remote area was part of civilization. This road lasted about twenty-one miles, and at the very end of it was the front gate of Angola Prison.

Twelve prisoners, all Black — Including Steve, Duck, Jellybean, and me — chained together, stepped from the van. Passing through the gate, I saw a large, two-story building before me. I got the impression that someone had built up sand mounds and placed large cardboard boxes upon them in the shape of a huge T. This area was (and is) known as "The Hill" because it sits higher than the rest of the prison grounds. In this building was the prison hospital, death row, and CCR (closed cell restriction), the prison's maximum security unit.

Entering the prison, I got the impression that I had been hurled backwards, into the past. The speech, the manner, and the actions of the prison's keepers was indicative of a former period; their utter contempt towards the kept was a well-oiled science, which the likes of Simon Legree (the slave owner in *Uncle Tom's Cabin*) would have envied. I also noticed a number of other dudes dressed differently than those I knew to be the keepers and the kept, in khaki uniforms. As I was being processed into the penitentiary that day, I learned of their function.

Those dudes dressed in khaki outfits were also prisoners. Their function was the backbone, so to speak, of the prison; over 90 percent of the prison's security rested upon their egos and their shoulders. The "khaki-backs," as they were called, shouldered this responsibility like well-trained hound-dogs, as if their very existence depended upon it. They internalized the keepers' wishes with zeal. They manned most of the towers, guarded work lines, assisted in (and initiated) beatings, and headed the chases whenever some unfortunate attempted to flee. They had the run of the penitentiary, and the majority of them bore as much, or more, contempt for their fellow prisoners as the keepers did.

After being processed, I was sent to Camp F, where the newly arrived were kept for approximately thirty days. This period in the reception center covered both quarantine and orientation for the "fresh fishes." It didn't take long for me to realize that everything centered around work. Work was the prison's theme, its cardinal rule. As the keepers put it, "ev'ry swingin' dick" was required to work, except for those locked down twenty-three hours a day for security reasons and thus denied the privilege to earn two and a half cents an hour (big deal!).

After about three days in the reception center, we were called to the camp's kitchen for continued initiation and orientation. After filing into the building, we came face to face with a Captain of the keepers. Without preliminaries or diplomacy, the man began, "I just summoned y'all heah for a few minutes to let y'all know a few facts." He paused, took his time, and gazed at the forty-odd faces in the room in a slow, deliberate manner. Continuing, he said, "Some of y'all is goin' in population soon; some of you will get jobs (which meant out of the field), but most of you will go to the field. Y'all work ever' day but Saturday and Sunday. During cane (cutting) season some of y'all will work those days, too, until cane season is ovah. Refusin' to work is a serious charge, and we don't tolerate it. If'n you refuse, we got a place to send ya." He then reached into his back pocket, pulled out a handkerchief and blew his nose (which sounded like a horn), and asked, "Do I make myself clear?" After seeing a few bowing heads in assent, he went on, "Y'all come heah to do time, and by golly, y'all gon' to do it if'n we have to kill ya and bury ya ovah thar (pointing) on Point Lookout. While yo're heah you do yore own time, mind yore own business. Politicians will not be tolerated and no instigatin' is allowed." Then he turned and left us there, musing over what he had said.

Angola covered about 18,000 acres at the time. Scattered over this vast acreage were many smaller prisons, commonly referred to as "outcamps." Then there was the main prison, built in 1957, referred to by a variety of names: "The Walk," "New Prison," or the "Big Yard." It consisted of cell blocks (which, at the time, had a status between medium and maximum security), sixteen medium security dormitories, and an equal number of minimum security dormitories. Of the more than 4,000 convicts held at the time, the main prison housed more than half.

On the day I was classified, they assigned me to the main prison; my living quarters were Hickory-4 and my work assignment, Farm Line #7. I walked into the dormitory, which consisted of about sixty beds, all neatly made. There were two people inside. One face, I could put no name to; the other belonged to my uncle Henry.

I knew Henry was still in prison, but until then, not where. He had long ago stopped writing the family. I had figured I would run into him before long, but I had no idea it would be so soon. I was glad to see him, for it had been more than six years since we had last cast eyes upon each other. It was a pity, though, that we had to meet in prison. He and I didn't really know each other; we were strangers, despite having the same blood flowing through our veins. That day, we set out anew to become brothers and friends; in time, despite our age differences, we became peers.

Just before noon, the field hands and other workers began pouring up the walk, going to their respective dormitories to await the count clearance before the noon meal. Entering the dining hall, looking into the sea of black faces, I saw many that were familiar from the reformatory. Many others from the reformatory who weren't at Angola that day would eventually show up another day.

October was cane-cutting season — two and a half cents an hour. In the months ahead, not only would I learn to cut cane, but also learn blading, ditching, quarter-draining, hoeing stubble, and a number of other tasks I had never before heard of, nor thought of doing.

During sugar cane season, all attention was focused on cane-cutting by the keepers. They were enthusiastic about it, and we prisoners were expected to show just as much enthusiasm and many did.

I had never cut cane before, but I was expected to learn that day. I did. There were old hands on the headland, whose job it was to count off rows and set others in, four to a set and offer a "lick to fresh fishes." A lick was simply showing a new man how it was done very quickly, then leaving him on his own. Any problems the new man had after getting that first lick would be solved by the foreman, whose options were to call a patrol and send the man to the dungeon, or write up a disciplinary report, charging him with "dragging ass" (malingering).

Many of those who received disciplinary reports and were dungeonized for work offenses weren't malingering. They just couldn't do any better. Even veteran prisoners, after years of trying, never did. But no one was exempt where work was concerned, especially during the sugar cane season, which had all the hallmarks of chattel slavery, even to the two weeks off once the cane-cutting season was over, usually in December.

While it is true that, at the time, Blacks made up nearly two-thirds of the prison population, the contrast between the number of white work lines and Black work lines was stark. Blacks had some twenty-odd lines, while whites had about three. Even during sugar cane season, white lines were rarely seen working. Whenever we did come across them, on a certain day, in a certain cut, the next day would find them still in the same cut. Out of the fields, the numbers were reversed. Classification clerks, parole clerks, pardon board clerks, hospital clerks, and whatever other clerks were needed for the main prison to function, these positions were reserved for whites only. The prison boasted of only one Black clerk, a protestant chaplain's clerk. The all-white administration that ran Angola was overtly conciliatory towards the white inmates, and showed unrestrained contempt for Blacks.

Though only eighteen when entering Angola, I felt much older. And thanks (no thanks) to a rough street life, I felt I had paid my dues. My years of triumphs and trials had left me arrogant; I had what was called a "pretty ego." I had the attitude that life had nothing more to offer me, nor could life get anything from me, for I had nothing. But in spite of feeling I had nothing, I felt I had done it all, and should I perish the next moment, so be it. I wouldn't be missing out on anything. For the first few months after my arrival, I abandoned all caution where my fellow prisoners were concerned: a most dangerous approach at the time, for Angola was like a war zone, where my "devil may care" attitude and approach were mirrored hundreds of times in other prisoners who didn't care either. If I somehow had the misconception that I was setting a pattern, I was sadly mistaken, for I was only allowing myself to follow an already-set pattern, established by those who came before me. In this war zone, a day didn't pass without casualties. I witnessed young men, the flower of the Black Nation, dying for naught at the hands of their brethren, who delighted in slaying them, and saw their deeds as noble. It was indeed fratricide in practice, but with "bloods wasting bloods" it was more akin to suicide, self-destruction. My fellow "bloods" and I were caught up in this disastrous pattern, which no doubt would have inevitably destroyed me, had not Henry, concerned for my well-being, intervened. His seasoned wisdom (gained from years of experience) persuaded me to move with more caution . . . to care. So I "lambed up" and survived.

After cleaning up my act, I needed something to replace what I had cast off. A void developed, and deepened. Feeling "clean and empty," I attempted to fill this void by reading. At first I read everything I could get my hands on, the Bible included. And then (for a while) I ceased reading anything but the Bible. Thus, I was introduced to religion and Christianity as never before. It touched that part of me in which I had previously felt nothing or which no one could touch. And in time, I internalized Christianity, made it my life style.

I had always been mindful of the imbalances of the society in which I subsisted—the unanswered questions that left me disoriented and wanting. At this time in my life, I needed something to justify my acceptance of this slavery-like condition, both in society and in prison. I wanted to give reasons why society was set up the way it was for people of African descent; to give reasons why my keepers acted the way they did; to give reasons why I (we) shouldn't wage fervent struggle (but pray) in response; to give reasons why I (we) should remain passive in the wake of so much persecution, and turn the other cheek. The Bible, while it didn't answer all questions, gave reasons. And this made life, as it was, more acceptable.

Armed with my new outlook, I engaged only in what I saw as constructive living, forsaking worldly aspirations. I took to Christianity with a fervor; after studying and learning about it, I taught it, ate with it, and slept with it. And for a while, put nothing before or after it.

After six months had passed, I got a new job assignment working in the kitchen. I met a guy (we became friends, of sorts) called "Cap Pistol." Cap was also from New Orleans, and was noted among prisoners and "free folks" alike for his culinary talents. He made some of the best pecan candy I'd ever tasted. Cap learned of my interest and shared his secrets with me. Since then, I have added my own twist to making the candy, which I perfected while in prison. Instead of calling my candy pralines, I call them "freelines" (thanks to a lady named Lorrie who coined the word). I have been making them since my release . . .

Those early years in Angola saw me become one of the cooks in the main kitchen, working along with Henry, with lots of leisure time. Still later, with the release of the chaplain's clerk, I was reassigned to that job and given a trustee's status, for all it was worth. During the two years or more that I was around Henry, I learned a lot from him about the art of boxing. At the time, he was reputed to be the "best boxer on the river." I wanted some of that. So he and I began my training and he taught me, as he put it, everything he knew. When he had finished teaching me, I continued to teach myself. At that time it was my desire to go back into the "free world" and engage in boxing.

Being in the described state of conformity — that is, seeing my condition as being decreed — had its benefits. The time passed quickly. 1964 came around, and soon after that, Henry was released. Later that same year, I was brought before the parole board and missed it. Six months later they brought me back, and this time I made it. After a few more months of red tape, after more than four years of imprisonment, they released me in November 1965. I was twenty-two years old.

CHAPTER 17

UPON MY RELEASE, NOT ONLY DID I FEEL I had accomplished something attitudinal and emotional, but I also felt a physical accomplishment. Coming to Angola, the war zone, and leaving it alive was indeed an accomplishment . . . Even after "lambing up," leaving Angola wasn't promised to anyone.

Point Look Out, one of the prison's gravesites, is filled to capacity with the remains of prisoners who were killed or died there. They have two gravesites now. There were many incidents that I encountered that could have kept me there forever, but one in particular is worth mentioning. It happened about six months before I was released on parole. At one point I worked for the chaplain, clerking. This job allowed me to meet with incoming inmates, called fresh fishes, while they were held in quarantine before they were finally classified into their final living quarters. Many of these inmates, mostly first-timers, were glad to see a familiar face once they entered the general population, and I was always that familiar face because they had met me before.

That did not set too well with many of the old-timers, however, who had other designs and who saw my befriending fresh fishes as an impediment to "turning out" a weak inmate. "Turning out" was intimidating them and forcing them to have sex. Turning them into "gal-boys," which is what they called them. Raping them. That's what they did to guys who were weak. It just so happens that a person I had befriended was seen as weak, and I was standing in the way. So naturally I had to be moved, or at least be challenged.

By this time, January 1965, I had made parole and was anticipating my release. I had changed job assignments and I now worked in the kitchen. It was actually called the scurry, where you washed trays. I had to make sure that trays were clean and constant, to keep pace with the demand during chow. I also gathered them from tables. In the process of gathering trays on this particular morning and consumed by work I had temporarily stashed my knife.

By the way, lambing up does not mean one has to go unprotected without a knife. When more than two-thirds of the prisoners had them, it was common sense. On this morning, however, in stashing my knife I had broken the cardinal rule: if you had a knife, you kept it on you at all times. My antagonist on this morning had his'n. He had also made parole, and I did not know this. I also didn't know he had a beef against me until the morning it happened.

It was sudden. From the corner of my eyes I caught a shadow, and turning I saw the upraised arm with knife in hand come down, sinking deep into my exposed left shoulder. It was the only target he had because I had turned; he was aiming to stab me in the back. Turning toward my foe I saw the knife coming down again, slashing my skull and coming down into my right shoulder. I knew I was in a fight for my life, and weaponless I began to fight to save my life. All I could do was deflect most of the blows with my arm. When it was finally over, I was covered with blood. Walking to the point where a vehicle would transport me to the hospital, I managed to lose a lot of blood.

Now although I had lost all of this blood, I was never really out of it. I remember lying on the hospital table, deep in thought. I was brought back to reality when I heard one of the inmate hospital workers say "there are no vital signs," and he covered my face the way you would cover that of a deceased person. I realized they were talking about me, and I snatched the cover from my face . . .

Now in retrospect, I believe that he and I were both very fortunate to have made parole. He did not get charged with an offense and I didn't want him charged. In my mind at the time was only this thought: once I healed I would see him again, and one of us would never leave prison.

In any event, he left and I eventually left prison for the first time, and that is why I felt it to be an accomplishment to have left. This was November 1965.

Home, as I knew it, had long been destroyed, even before my going to the reformatory. Therefore, I had no home to go to. But the condition of my parole was that I would take up residence with Verna Mae, who had moved to New Orleans, east. In fact, most of the immediate family had moved to that area; my mother had always lived there. Robert, Houston, George, and James, who had by this time returned from Chicago, and Mary had become a part of the city's crowd. Henry, upon his release, had moved east to Philadelphia, leaving his family.

Mule still lived in Algiers and he was his same old self, except that he didn't drink anymore and walked with a cane due to a stroke. He now lived with a former neighbor, who was herself getting on in years. And what of Ellen? When I first went to prison, she had weighed heavily on my heart and mind. But with the prospect of a ten-year sentence before me, I had forced her back into the recesses of my consciousness and after my conversion, she was pushed even further away. When I was released from prison, she was only a memory. Our time had passed. And besides, I had locked gazes with the woman who would eventually become my wife . . .

When I first saw Clara, Clara who became my wife, it was as if I had known her all my life, as if we were only attempting to continue something that had started eons ago. Our attraction to each other was mutual. She had two lovely daughters from a previous relationship. With nothing standing in our way, and both professing Christian principles, we wed. I was working for a small construction company at the time. I was also training, and came to know a brief semi-pro boxing career under the name "Speedy King."

Clara, her youngest daughter, Marilyn, and I (with "Lil' Robert" on the way) took up residence in the uptown area. During this period, I saw a lot of my mother, who seemed better able to deal with her self-consciousness in my presence. As a result, we were able to get much closer. In the summer of 1966, she had to be hospitalized. I visited her regularly and my wife did likewise. Actually, my wife (twenty-two years old at the time) and my mother had known each other since my wife was a tot; after our marriage, which my mother readily sanctioned, they hit it off real good. They found humor in being in each other's company and I found humor in the fact that I had two women in my life both named Clara!

I never did find out the exact reason my mother had to be hospitalized, but I do know that it was related to her drinking and that the doctor, after releasing her, told her she *had* to stop drinking. As she had so many times before, she vowed she would stop. This vow she could never keep.

Less than a month later, she was dead.

At the wake, I met a lot of relatives I hadn't seen in years; some I had never before met. One of those was Clara's youngest daughter, my sister, Ella Mae. I was twenty-three years old.

Clara was not brought back to Gonzales, as Grandma, Grandpa, and Mama had been. Instead, a burial site was found in Providence Memorial Park, right off Airline Highway. Her remains are buried there.

In saying some final words for Clara, what can I say except that despite all, she was the one responsible for my being in this existence and, to a great degree, responsible for what I have become. Though I have a beef, a complaint, about my station in this life, I have no beef about the person I have become. Therefore, she accomplished her mission.

In spite of all that had occurred in my life, and in spite of all the "small inconsistencies" in my behavior, I had no problem identifying with the establishment and what it stood for. Not until the latter part of 1966, when the seeds of severance were implanted in my conscience, and the emotional tie I once felt for the American system began to fade . . .

In October of that year, while making my way home, after getting a lift from an acquaintance who had been driving down

South Claiborne Ave., we passed a parked car. It was dark but we were able to see inside — and inside was a white dude who appeared to be unconscious. We both became concerned, and, in spite of my having some reservations, I was glad when Boogie stopped his car, got out and walked back to check on the guy. I remained in the car and watched through the rear view mirror as he looked inside, checking for signs of life from the occupant. From where I was, it appeared that Boogie was talking to the dude, and I saw movement, which indicated that the man was okay. Boogie came back and said, "The dude is drunk, probably sleeping it off." With that he got in and we drove off. Within minutes we were surrounded by police cars, sirens wailing. Policemen jumped from their cars even before they had come to a stop, guns drawn, shouting "Get outta the car!" and "Reach for the sky!" (I immediately got a flashback to five years earlier.) We were frisked, handcuffed and unceremoniously placed in one of the police cars. An officer sent to check on the man in the car came back, saying, "He's okay, still drunk." Then he went to our car, gave it a superficial search, and came up with a watch from (as he said) "beneath the front seat." And just like that, we had us a robbery charge.

On the night we got caught in the police dragnet, we didn't know that they had the car under surveillance and were waiting for someone to approach. Being the good concerned citizens we thought ourselves to be, thinking that that dude needed help, we had approached the car and played into their hands. The police's official version of the incident was that they had spotted the drunk in the automobile and, instead of bringing him in, had left him there with a watch planted close by, waiting for someone to approach. The result was our arrest.

My version has been stated. Furthermore, I have no doubt whatsoever that the watch the police "found" under our front seat was planted there by the cop who searched the car. It was as clear a case of simple framing as I'd seen. I was able to make bail and was released that same night. The following day, knowing my innocence and wanting to do the right thing, I called my parole officer and informed him of this unusual turn of events. After hearing my version of what had transpired, he assured me that, if I was innocent, I had nothing to worry about. Then just before hanging up the phone, making it appear as an afterthought, he said, "Oh, Robert how about coming down to my office? I want to go over those details again; I want to make sure I've got them right." I didn't think anything odd about it. Assured I didn't have anything to worry about, like a good sheep going to slaughter, I made my way downtown to the P.O.'s office. I was told to wait a few minutes, and then he approached me, flanked by two other dudes, saying, "Robert, I am going to have to look into this matter further." He then produced a set of handcuffs and said, "In the meantime, I am going to have to place a hold on you."

I couldn't believe what was about to happen. I started to protest in the only way I knew how, by proclaiming my innocence. One of the dudes flanking him must have mistaken my protest as a form of resistance, for he gave me a cold stare and rearrested me, revoking both my bail and my parole. He drove to the parish prison himself. At this time, my wife was eight and one half months pregnant. Two weeks after my arrest, she bore a son, whom she named after me.

Six months after my arrest, I was still in jail, waiting to go to trial. It was about this time, the spring of 1967, that Clara came to visit me and told me that my sister, Mary, had died from pneumonia. She was twenty-seven years old. Through the efforts of my wife, I was allowed to attend a brief funeral service held in the church. Afterwards, they ushered me back to the prison without allowing me to attend the burial.

Mary's death was another in a series of losses for me. The harshness of her life-style had finally caught up with her. Right after my mother's death, I had looked for her, to bring her to the funeral; she was, after all, the eldest child. I found her in a pretty bad state. I tried to get her to come with me, but she said she would come by later. As it turned out, Mary hadn't shown up in time. When she did show, it was past 3:00 a.m. and the funeral parlor was closed for the night. The next day, about noon, when the procession was about to leave for the burial site, we found her sitting on the funeral parlor's step, weeping.

I was told by James at the brief service I attended for Mary, that she had "left the streets for good" before dying. I was glad of that. But what left a lasting impression upon me was her final gesture towards our mother, her weeping for her loss on the funeral parlor steps.

Eleven months later, I was still awaiting trial in the parish prison. By this time, I had made more than a dozen court appearances, supposedly going to trial, but no victim ever showed up. Each time I went, the district attorney had tried vainly to get me, along with Boogie, to plea bargain — that is, to cop-out to a lesser charge for which we would have received a small sentence and credit for time served, which would have probably put us on the street. That was the theory. But this theory couldn't apply to me, only to Boogie. I was on parole, and any conviction warranted an automatic revocation. Boogie, who could have taken the prosecution's offer six months earlier, had gallantly held out knowing that we both would be exonerated once we went to trial. But after nearly a year, his resolve was all used up. He went for the district attorney's offer and was released the same day. I went to court that day also and the district attorney moved to drop the case against me. The court granted his motion, and the case against me was dropped.

I was surprised. It looked like a victory. When the case against me was dropped, I was expecting to be released also. But that proved to be a vain hope, for I had been arrested with a felon who had been forced to plead to guilty to another felony. His guilty plea, though to a lesser charge, affected me as if I had pled guilty myself. The elaborate motion the prosecutor had made to the court to drop the case against me, and the court's subsequent granting it, was purely for show. It was all a cruel charade.

When it became clear that I wouldn't be released, I tried getting the eleven months I had been held counted, but to no avail. It was considered "dead time."

In September 1967, they returned me to prison to complete my original sentence. A few days after arriving back at Angola, I appeared before the Parole Board and had my parole "officially revoked." Shit! That was a laugh. So it hadn't been "officially" revoked nearly a year ago . . .

CHAPTER 18

THIS LAST MOVE BY THE STATE WAS LIKE water on a dying ember, smothering my already fading emotions and for the first time in my life, I stopped seeing ill-happenings as being decreed, and began to place the shoe on the foot where it belonged. I ceased subjecting myself blindly to the system and the powers-that-be. I was now primed for the education that eventually came.

Meanwhile, here I was, back in Angola knowing who was responsible for my being here, but not really understanding why. At this stage, causes and effects had little meaning. But I went about my prison activities suffering a lot less peacefully than I had the last time around; with the shadow of awareness came grief, and I would let nothing justify or moderate my grief this time around.

Initially, I worked in the field, but being an "old hand" and having a reputation as a cook, it didn't take me long to get a job in the Camp A kitchen.

Clara made infrequent visits; each time she came, she brought the children. I had first seen my son at my sister's funeral. He was a very small tot at the time. Children weren't allowed to visit at the parish prison, so I was unable to see him the whole time I was there. By the time his mother brought him to visit me at the penitentiary, he was almost two years old and, if I might add, quite receptive. So it was in the prison visiting room that my son and I first got acquainted.

Finally, the fifteen months I owed the state were behind me, and in January 1969, I was once again released from prison, discharged after serving almost nine of the original ten years.

When I was released from prison in January 1969, Angola was worse than it was in 1961. Murders — condoned and perpetuated by the prison officials — were rampant. Economic slavery, characterized by long hours of work for only pennies an hour, was the norm, as was sexual slavery, or the selling of "weakly" inmates into forced homosexuality for sexual exploitation.

While my wife Clara had made infrequent trips to Angola with Lil' Robert, as we called him, she and I were emotionally separated. Nevertheless, we made a half-hearted attempt to get back together. I even managed to get a job in the city's largest cemetery, receiving minimum wage.

Clara and I eventually separated for good. However, despite the separation, I managed to see my son on a regular basis. By this time, there wasn't much left of my immediate family. Mule, though plagued with health problems, was still hanging on. But while not much had changed regarding my family, I had begun to notice a mood shift in people old and young.

In my more than two years away, a change had taken place in society. One big leap forward seemed to have occurred. There were all kinds of fads, whims, and trends, due to technology. People clung to (and changed) trends as they changed their dress. But the thing that most caught my attention was the leap in consciousness that had taken place, seemingly overnight, in the psychology of Black people in America. This new mood was widespread in New Orleans. This new state of mind, which eventually became known as "Black Consciousness," had replaced (or had begun replacing) the old treadmill mentality that Blacks had of forever imitating and wanting to be like white folks. Now everybody who was Black, even those with just a "trace of Black blood," wanted to be Black and Proud. Even many of those Blacks who had been "passing" for years wanted to come back to the blackness they had previously denied.

I loved it. And like so many others, after being caught up in it, I accepted it as completely as I could, given my level of understanding at the time. I was Black and Proud.

Though we no longer related as husband and wife, Clara and I didn't put too much distance between us. We sort of understood each other's needs. Lil' Robert was about three and a half years old by this time, and I was determined to see that he not suffer the poverty I had suffered at his age. Those basic necessities of life that had seemed like luxuries to me at his age (when I was fortunate enough to get them) would be things he would take for granted. I would see to that.

I didn't have any major problem with finding employment as before, but, as before, the pay was minimal. To supplement my income, I began once more to engage in semi-pro bouts, fighting as "Speedy King" in the limelight of the likes of Al (Alvin) Phillips, Jerry Pelligrini, and Percy Pugh. I was at the gym every chance I got and fighting whenever I could on whatsoever card came up. But with the more than two year's interruption, my boxing had suffered a major setback. Many of my former sparmates had gone on, in my absence, to become local favorites, and some enjoyed national ratings. I had a lot of catching up to do, for I was still striving in the semi-pro ratings. But I didn't catch up. I stayed with boxing a while longer, but I began to lose some of my interest and began to falter in the discipline it took to be a fighter. Boxing was a sport I loved, and loved doing. But not wanting to make a mockery of myself, I made a strategic retreat.

CHAPTER 19

THE YEAR WAS 1970. I HAD BEEN ON THE street for a year, managing to provide for myself and Lil' Robert, whom I saw regularly. Then my destiny caught up with me again.

According to a police affidavit dated February 18, 1970, an alleged robbery was committed by two male subjects. The alleged victim said that one of the perpetrators was about forty years old, but she could not identify him. The other, a younger man, she could, and eventually did, identify. The man she identified was subsequently arrested and charged with the crime.

Some two weeks after the incident, detectives converged upon my uptown residence without a warrant, forced their way inside, held me at gunpoint and methodically ransacked my dwelling. Their plundering naturally turned up a gun. I was told I was wanted for questioning in a robbery. They then took me to police headquarters and booked me.

Later, I was sent to the parish prison, placed on the same tier with Wortham Jones Jr., who had been previously identified as one of the perpetrators. When we learned that we had been arrested for the same charge, we talked. Jones said, "Man, these cops are only feelin' in the wind, chasing ghosts; they ain't got nothin' on me or you." I knew they didn't have anything on me, but I wondered how they could have tied me in with him? How had I become his forty-year-old accomplice at the age of twenty-eight? I found the whole thing to be rather bizarre. Even more so when, after about three weeks, my state-appointed attorney came to me with an offer from the D.A.'s office — if I pled guilty to the charge, the district attorney would see to it that I got only fifteen years! Naturally, I refused.

Not having the money to make the exorbitant bond placed upon me ($50,000!) I had to be content with waiting it out. I was eager and ready to go to trial, but knowing a little of the inner workings of the judicial system, I knew my wait could turn into a very long one.

In my talks with Jones, what I didn't know and what he chose not to tell me was that almost immediately after the alleged crime was committed, police had shown nine mug-shots to the victim. (It was, and probably still is, customary for police to show photos to victims of recently released prisoners.) After viewing the photos, the victim had identified only Wortham Jones Jr. The police had then arrested Jones and given him the usual third-degree (their trademark) and forced him to select a photo (his testimony at trial). The photo Jones had selected was mine. This had given the police the "probable cause" needed to arrest me and hold me in jail for nine days without charging me. During those nine days, police made frequent trips back to the victim, urging, coercing and coaching her telling her that Jones had "admitted" I was his accomplice. So the victim, who hadn't previously identified me as being one of the perpetrators, became convinced that I was. And the rest is history . . .

At the trial some three months later, the victim was convinced, beyond any doubt, that I was the "forty-year-old man" who had accompanied Jones in robbing her. My defense countered, "Look at him! The defendant is only in his mid-twenties, and could pass for twenty; how do you account for that?" The fact that she couldn't account for it made no difference. Her in-court identification was all that mattered, all that was needed to satisfy the law.

That day in court held many surprises for me. But the most startling, the most unexpected, was yet to come.

The prosecutor, attempting to administer the *coup de grace*, called Jones to the stand, to be a witness for the state. I was not surprised, since I already knew about his role in my being arrested. I knew it was all lies, so I was barely listening as Jones took the stand and admitted, under oath, that he had pulled the robbery. The prosecutor then asked him about his accomplice; was he now seated in the courtroom? The room was quiet, and when Jones's voice broke the silence with an emphatic "No!" it became quieter. The prosecutor looked at the judge in panic, then turned back to Jones and said, "Would you repeat your answer?" "No, my accomplice ain't here," said Jones. The prosecutor's face went white, even whiter, that is. "What? You don't know Robert Wilkerson? He wasn't with you on that robbery?" To that Jones replied, "I don't know Robert Wilkerson and he wasn't with me on no robbery." Then Jones went into a loud and angry diatribe, telling the court that it was looking at "a case and victim of police brutality." He then began pointing to scars that he said had been inflicted on him by police, at one time or another. When he was arrested for the robbery in question, he told the court, the police had beaten him while showing him mug shots (mine included), asking him which of the men in the photographs were his accomplices. He took as much torture as he could before finally picking one of the pictures at random as his "accomplice." Further testimony by Jones revealed that the police had then drawn up a "confession" and had forced him to sign it. When he finished testifying, he said to the district attorney, "Look, man, if the police had shown me your picture and asked me was you the one with me on that robbery, I probably would have said yes."

At this point, had the district attorney really been interested in the proper administration of justice, he would have, with the consent of the trial judge, declared the proceeding a mistrial. Instead, he chose to continue the sham. However, my hopes had begun to soar. I felt that the truth would determine the outcome of the trial. And the truth, I knew, was on my side.

There were other witnesses called who had been at the place when it was robbed. None, however, could link me to the crime. And I had witnesses to testify about my whereabouts at the approximate time the robbery allegedly occurred.

The trial ended that night with the prosecutor urging the jurors not to believe Wortham Jones Jr. "He is a liar!" he said in resounding tones. About two hours after leaving, the jury reentered the courtroom. I was tense with anticipation, knowing I would be freed. Tense moments also passed for my friends and relatives.

With the jury seated, the judge asked if they had reached a verdict. "Yes, your honor," replied the foreman. "Well," said the judge — smiling all the while — "let the court hear the verdict." The foreman said, "We, the jury, find the defendant guilty as charged." I sat there, transfixed with awe, terrified at the abuse of power I had just witnessed. The feeling then changed to indignation. I focused my anger on the jury. How could they, I thought, after all the evidence to the contrary? I then saw what "friend of the court" really meant. I learned what the district attorney had known all along. He knew he had a jury who, in the majority, were friends of the court.

I must, however, give credit where credit is due. All jurors aren't so easily persuaded. Two of them at my trial — one Black and one white — when the jury was polled, expressed their opinion in a manner that left me no doubt they were in dissent with their fellow-jurors: "Not guilty, absolutely not!" and "Not guilty, no way!"

I sat there in the aftermath, bathed in revulsion, while the prosecutor shook the hand of each individual juror, grinning like a wolf while doing so; the judge, from his bench, thanked them for doing such a "splendid job," a broad smile etched on his face.

Due to years of suffering, privation, and other hardships, a sophistication — commonly called "knowing the game" — has developed among subjects in America. This is nature's way of balancing, her way of making it up to those downtrodden individuals.

While all subjects ("subject" is here used interchangeably with African-American, but in a broader sense, it can refer to all people who are victimized by the system) aren't exactly players, all, beyond doubt, are aware of the game. The most aware are the most dispossessed, the lumpen, the so-called "criminal element." The lumpen subject, by decree of the powers-that-be, is cut off from the economic security enjoyed by others and must therefore put his or her knowledge of the game into full play just to survive. With cunning, developed over a long period of having to struggle, he/she must extend and stretch himself/herself beyond acceptable boundaries. To him/her there is a justifiable self-respect — even a challenge — found in playing out of bounds, pitting his or her wits against the system, getting over wherever, whenever and however he/she can.

At the same time, getting over on the establishment never means collaborating with police or other enforcers. In 1970, at the time of my trial, many lumpen subjects of the day took pride in seeing that the "game" was played straight and one of the ways of playing it straight was never ratting on a fellow subject. And so, as you can imagine, I had a difficult time putting Jones into perspective. For long moments after the guilty verdict, I was killing mad with him; I branded him a collaborator and a rat. But then I began to think: how could he have ratted on me when I wasn't his actual accomplice? In spite of feeling used, hurt, and being the biggest loser at this bizarre throw of the dice, I had to conclude that Jones had stretched the "game" as far as he could, in an attempt to stay loyal to the code. The way he saw it, by selecting one of the photos the police showed him, he was leading them away from his true accomplice. Plus, the man in the mug shot wouldn't be in any real danger of being convicted because he didn't look at all like the man who was actually with him. To Jones, this was all a part of getting over on the system.

After perceiving all of this, I couldn't stay killing mad with Jones. This is why after being returned to jail, I was able to restrain myself when he came up to me and said, "Man, I'm sorry. Ain't no way in the world those people should have found you guilty. I just picked you knowin' they couldn't convict you, that you'd beat the rap, man. You didn't look nuthin' like the dude man, nuthin' like the dude!"

I understood Jones's logic, but I didn't tell him this. I still felt the need to be killing mad with him; and although I wasn't, I wanted him to think I was. So I didn't say anything to him.

In the final analysis, my only beef with Jones was that he had not made me aware of this months earlier. Had he done so, my lawyer might have been able to somehow alter the circumstances in my favor. No, I wasn't angry at Jones anymore. He had told the truth at trial, and it wasn't he who had twisted the facts to find me guilty. The legal system had only proven what I had already begun to feel: that it ultimately cares little about guilt or innocence, especially of Black subjects. Its main concern is to obtain a conviction, to close the books and "clear" the case. In a process such as this, one can be morally innocent, but legally guilty.

Later that night, lying in my bunk, my whole life flashed before me. I refused to direct my anger toward Jones, a fellow victim. Instead, I became angry (and am to this day) at the "justice" system, its deliberate wanton deficiency and gullibility.

Thinking about my past re-awakened something within me. Remembering my years with my father, a connection emerged. Just as I had felt overwhelmed in Hillary's house by his unfairness towards me, I now felt overwhelmed by the system and its injustices. For the first time since being captured, I thought of escape. "That's my way out, my way of striking back," I thought. My thoughts and actions would meet, embrace as theory and practice should do. And to *not* do what I felt needed to be done would be something akin to a betrayal to my new maturity, my new hard-earned awakening. But most of all, I knew that should I remain neutral in the wake of this new consciousness, it would be a betrayal of my sanity. I now felt psychologically whole, as one might feel who had been afflicted with a perpetual oozing sore, which had abruptly dried up as a result of getting the proper medication.

Two weeks later I was brought back to court and sentenced to thirty-five years in prison. This meant nothing to me, for as I have said, the system no longer had any moral hold on me. After the sentencing, the state's appointed attorney gave his notice of appeal. That was only a formality, one in which I wouldn't participate. I would "appeal" all right, but the type of appeal I had in mind would be far removed from tradition and formality.

As it turned out, there were other brothers in jail who also felt this need to *appeal* to no one but themselves, where freedom was concerned. Together we proceeded to plan. Circumstances did not allow us to plan beyond the escape, which was only known to a few of us, because of possible collaborators within our midst. We kept it a secret until the last minute. Of the sixty-odd prisoners living on the tier in squalid, dehumanizing conditions who now had a chance to make their bid for freedom, only about a third chose to do so after the way had been cleared by those of us who planned.

Of the twenty-odd who did make the break, only three actually escaped. I was one of those three.

Most were apprehended within minutes. They had actually made it out of the prison, but weren't able to make themselves "invisible" in time. All of them suffered intense torture at the hands of the New Orleans police and prison deputies, who felt embarrassed and humiliated because of the escape. All were charged with new crimes (charges later dropped). The saddest note came some six hours after the jailbreak, when one of the brothers — Pulpwood, who had helped in the original plan — was spotted by a prison deputy, cornered, and killed. The deputy, also a "brother," was promoted to sergeant.

A week after the escape, there were only two of us still at large. A day or two into the second week, the other brother negotiated his own capture, and that left one. Me.

I stayed invisible for nearly two weeks before I was informed on (agents later told me) by a fellow subject who saw, recognized, and reported me to my enemies. So in June 1970, four months after the ordeal had begun and exactly one month after my trial and conviction, and subsequent escape, I was once again in captivity. I was charged with aggravated escape, and later brought back to court and sentenced to an additional eight years in prison.

CHAPTER 20

NOW BACK IN JAIL, I PAID MORE ATTENTION to current events: the face of America was undergoing a major transformation, especially where African-Americans were concerned. I began to feel myself a part of something whole, something big, something I could not define at the moment. One day, while watching the small television in the hall through the bars, an announcer cut into the regular programming, informing the viewers that a group of Black militants — males and females — had barricaded themselves in an apartment complex located in the lower Ninth Ward and were "shooting it out with the police." This caught my attention: it was something unprecedented in the city of New Orleans and as each scene unfolded, the kinship I felt with the group — whoever it was — grew.

Later I learned that the militants in the house called themselves "The National Committee to Combat Fascism," or NCCF. Still later, I learned that they were actually members of the Black Panther Party.

I had already been on the verge of "awakening," and the emergence of the Black Panther Party in New Orleans completed this awakening. The group, twelve in all, miraculously suffered no casualties. All were arrested and housed in the New Orleans Parish Prison. I was fortunate to meet most of the group, consisting of nine males and three females, who managed to communicate with their male counterparts in spite of being held in another section of the facility. These females also communicated with other prisoners besides their comrades. It was through this prison communication system that I met Cathy (or "Top

Cat"), Leah, and Elaine (also known as "E-Baby"). Top Cat was a source of strength to many of the prisoners, and she was my greatest inspiration. In her letters to me, she uttered the Party's doctrine as if she had written it herself and her in-depth knowledge of Marxism was second to none. She was fully dedicated and conducted herself as if she were in a hurry to accomplish an important mission. She remained true throughout her confinement. During my years of incarceration, I often wondered what ever happened to Cathy. Upon my release, I learned that she had become an "ancestor," dying in a Midwestern city, alone, abandoned by the very people that she was willing to die for. Other females affiliated with the New Orleans Black Panther Chapter (with the exception of Betty Toussaint Powell, who was shot in a second raid by policemen acting as priests, but survived and later came to jail) escaped jail time. They were Marion H. Brown and Mary (who later became members of the Party), and Linda who remained a "community worker." These three had become affiliated with the Black Panther Party while students at Tulane University. Joined by Shirley Duncan (the youngest Pantherette at the time) and Althea Francois, these women zealously visited Party members and would-be members who were imprisoned at the time. Even to this day, Marion and Althea are still visiting imprisoned Panthers . . .

Ronald Ailsworth was one of nine Panthers arrested during the first police raid on the New Orleans chapter. If inspiration is likened to a two-sided coin (and held in my hand) with Top Cat's face appearing on one side, then Ron's face undoubtedly graces the other. It was Ron, working alongside Alton Edwards (or "E. D.") and others, who helped secure the safety of those inside the house and thwarted a massacre by the police. It was Ron's knowledge of and revelations about the Party that ultimately committed me to their concepts. The keepers had separated him from the original group of Panthers, who were kept on tier C–1. Ron was sent to C-3, where I was kept. Shortly thereafter, another Panther, Shelly Batiste (now an ancestor) was arrested and also sent to C-3. It was through Ron, though, that I was introduced to the Party's teachings and Platform. We began to hold political discussions, and it was through these discussions that I grasped the historical plight of Blacks and other poor people in America. I also learned the art of collectivity, and the means and methods of struggle . . .

The conditions in the prison were horrible. The tiers, originally built to house forty-eight prisoners, were holding twice that many. Toilets ran all night, and water, infested with feces, would run into the hallways where prisoners had to sleep. Louse-infested mattresses and covers were given to us. Huge rats, coming up from the sewers, challenged prisoners for their food — which was inadequate anyway, both in quality and quantity, having no nutritional value. Many prisoners were held in these sordid conditions for two years or more, without being charged, tried, or sentenced. This practice later prompted the Panther brothers housed on tier C-1 to resort to drastic measures in order to rectify this. Two deputies were held hostage, which got the attention of prison officials and the public at large.

On C-3, where I resided, we tried to negotiate with the keepers to no avail; the practice of dehumanizing us continued. Ultimately, we engaged in a hunger strike in which several hundred prisoners participated. Ron, Shelly, and I were singled out as agitators and sent to another facility that housed federal prisoners. There we continued our political discussions and protests, educating those brothers who were there before us.

After about six months, they returned me back to the parish prison. I met more members of the New Orleans Black Panther chapter, those caught up in the second police raid. Among them was Charles "Chucky" Scott (now an ancestor) who was responsible for my becoming an official member of the Party. I also met Harold ("Poison") Holmes (also an ancestor) and Donald Guyton, now Malik Rahim, who remains an advocate for justice and prisoners rights. He spearheaded the efforts to garner support for Herman Wallace, Albert Woodfox, and myself. In time, we became known as the Angola 3.

Contrary to what the power structure would have us believe, the Black Panther Party's ideology was not cut from the block of gangsterism. Rather, its ideology defined the overall Black experience in America — past and current — and provided Blacks and other oppressed peoples in America with alternative ways of resisting American-style repression politically, economically, racially and/or socially — by any means necessary — as advocated by one of the Party's benefactors, Malcolm X.

The Party recognized the myth of democracy, particularly where Blacks were concerned, and set itself up from among the individuals downtrodden by the system. The goal was always for the people to be their own vanguard. It boasted a sound political objective. Its main points were: *We want freedom! We want justice! Land, Bread, Education, Housing. An end to police brutality and occupation of the Black communities.* The Party took pride in and embraced nationalism or nationhood, where Blacks were concerned and it advocated internationalism, where oppressed peoples of the world were concerned. The Party saw revolution as the only means of altering the existing gap between the haves and the have-nots. I could not help but embrace its concepts, then and now.

Since that day, the Black Panther Party has become defunct. Over the years, its members have been imprisoned and murdered. Its ideology has been subverted. In the Black Panther Party, Blacks had a truly legitimate political representative and defender for the first time. This is not to say that the Party was the only legitimate political party that Blacks have ever known, but it is saying that the Party was more truly legitimate than any other. This is because of its willingness to implement means to back up its political ideology.

Malcolm X recognized the fact that the same conditions that made a Black political organization necessary, also made it necessary that it be capable of defending itself against the system. Without this capability, no political structure, anywhere, can claim to be a truly legitimate representative of anyone.

Meeting those members of the Black Panther Party during the time it was in full swing was a plus for me. I was able to put the happenings of my individual life into a broader perspective.

My awareness only added to my determination to escape those who held me unjustly, against my will. But it wasn't to be. By this time, a number of other inmates and myself were being housed at the parish prison annex, formerly known as the First Precinct police station where, in the past, city policemen had satisfied their sadistic appetites on mostly Black subjects. At the present time, though, it housed both federal and state prisoners, and had the distinction of being manned (most times) by segments of all law enforcement agencies, even the army. Except for court appearances and a few minutes for showering, we were locked in cells all day, harassed and provoked most of the time by sadistic guards. After months of this type of treatment, I and the two other inmates (now deceased) in the cell with me were fed up with it. There wasn't much we could do except throw a little abuse of our own, and small pieces of bathing soap. One would have thought we had murdered the president and all his men. The warden arrived with a dozen or so of his goons, all carrying night-sticks, shields, iron pipes; a few were even brandishing knives. Our cell door was opened and we were ordered to "Come out, or be drugged out." I looked at that warden like he was crazy. If he thought I was going to step into a sea of revenge-crazed men brandishing all that weaponry, he was crazy. I decided to take my chances by letting them drag me out. The two other bloods in the cell held those same sentiments. So we left it on them to come into the cell. And come they did.

All the deputies, crazed as they were, crowded into the cell at one time, eager to get in on the beating. With the cell only six by nine, they could hardly achieve that goal effectively. In the melee, a deputy was stabbed, presumably by one of his fellow deputies. As one might guess, the blame was attributed to us.

We were beaten and dragged from the cell to the dungeon, where we were beaten some more. By this time, deputies who had gone off duty were called back in to "help stop an escape attempt" and get in on the action. In the meantime, the wounded deputy had already been taken to the hospital for treatment.

The incident had begun around 7:00 p.m. By midnight, the three of us were in the dungeon, handcuffed and shackled to the bars, bruised, swollen and feeling somewhat defeated for the moment. Deputies came to the cell, unshackled one of the men from the bars, and took him to the hospital. I later learned that they administered more beatings to him on the way.

Around 3:00 a.m., in the wee small hours of the morning, my turn came. At the time, I had no idea what had happened to my fellow inmate. I was pretty banged up, so when they told me that the warden had ordered them to take me to the hospital, I had no argument with that. I really needed my many wounds attended.

The brother of the wounded deputy and another deputy were assigned to drive me to the hospital. Neither ever said a word to me. Still shackled, I was placed in the back of a police van, lying upon its floor, cuffed. A few blocks from the jail, in a secluded area, we stopped. Lights out. I braced myself as best I could. Within seconds the back of the van opened. Enter the brother of the wounded deputy, brandishing a three-foot tire iron. What followed was what always follows when a cop is allowed to vent his rage and racism unrestrained. By the time we reached the hospital, I was even more of a mess than before.

The hospital staff had been prepared for my coming. I was the criminal who had "nearly killed a deputy on duty while attempting to escape." I didn't expect nor did I receive anything but the required perfunctory treatment reserved for persons of ill repute. Then I was returned to jail to nurse my own wounds and heal the best way I could.

The three of us were charged with the incident and each of us faced an additional ten years in prison. The way it turned out, though, I was the only one to receive more time. A deal was made that if one of us would "cop out" (plead guilty), it would set the others free. So without ever getting to the bottom of who it was who had really wounded the deputy, the matter was settled with a plea bargain. I received an additional seven years to run concurrently with the time I had recently received for the escape.

CHAPTER 21

DURING MY NEARLY TWO-YEAR STAY AT the New Orleans Parish Prison, awaiting the results of my appeal, tragedy struck. It began in late 1970 with a visit from Clara, my wife. I learned that my four year old son, Lil' Robert, had developed a tumor on his brain. The doctors had told her that his life couldn't be saved. He would die within six months. This news left me wasted, weeping within and without, but still hopeful that the doctors were wrong and that he, my son, would live. But that wasn't to be. Lil' Robert didn't live. Still approaching the tender age of five, my son passed from this existence, taking a part of me with him.

The death of my son was the final catalyst; it served as the final consciousness raiser for me. I now felt the need to know. That knowledge was a responsibility of the first magnitude and my personal object of study would be my enemy, the system.

In studying and learning of my enemy, I also learned of myself, my place in history. In learning of my place in history, I rediscovered my long-lost humanity. Individuality was replaced with the need for unity. Certainty replaced uncertainty.

I saw that all are expendable at the system's whim. I saw how my mother, her mother and her mother's mother before her suffered. I saw past generations of my forefathers stripped from their homeland, brought, by force, to these shores in chains. They were stripped of all sense of responsibility; their only obligation belonged to their servitude. I saw mothers become the predominant parental figure within the slave unit, while fathers did not know their offspring. I was able to put some of my father

Hillary's actions into perspective. Hillary, born into a white world and dominated at every turn, felt the need himself to dominate.

I saw the rising crisis of the late fifties and early sixties emerging — education, patriotism and deception being the main tools used to manipulate the masses. The word *education* became a banner for the young; you had to "get an education" if you wanted to "get a 'decent' job." At that time, getting an education meant getting a high school diploma. With that, you could be hired as a clerk, a drugstore attendant, or maybe even a secretary. But as time went on, a pile-up occurred. Many did indeed get their high school diplomas, but a job they did not get.

The system had to boost the educational standards. A high school diploma was no longer enough; you had to go to college and get a degree. Those bearing a high school diploma were relegated to a work bracket formerly designated to those who had not finished high school. And still, many of those with college degrees soon met the same fate of the bearers of diplomas; many found themselves still jobless. What followed was a snowballing of unemployment and under-employment, with people of African descent leading the pace. High school dropouts, and those having no former education whatsoever, found themselves outside the system completely, "carrying stick" as Buddy had once said.

Many recognized the deception of the system. Some felt helpless to do anything about it, and languished in poverty. Others found contentment in living off their wits, by any means necessary. Quite a few of the upper middle class youths, much closer to the system than most, took the matter more personally. They bypassed revolution and turned "hippie," rejecting, for a while, the mores of the system.

Although the promise of education had initially succeeded in blunting the will for change, there were now many "educated" people, but no jobs. Nearly all the young by this time had begun to see the hypocrisy of the system, and the situation became potentially explosive. The youth had taken to the streets, demonstrating, protesting, and burning. The system forestalled some protest in the form of federal grants to aid cities and states, along with other token approaches amounting to welfare. It augmented its already existing police state at a rapid pace. New police and defense agencies were created, and those already existing were increased in manpower.

It became clear to me that, in spite of all its efforts to quell unrest, the system still found itself faced with the problem of the unemployed and underemployed. Enough prisons could never be built to accommodate this vast number of people. So the system developed a way to appeal to the loyalty of its inhabitants. It put up banners to America the Beautiful, it spouted slogans of "love it or leave it." And it sent the young and the restless — therefore the most dangerous element — to fight an unjust war in South East Asia.

The war cut down on the demand for jobs, and took many of the young from the streets and soup lines of America. I saw the war absorbing two or more generations of youths. Many would never return alive from Vietnam. Many of those who managed to survive and return would join the future ranks of the unemployed. Far too many would wind up in prison, languishing there until forgotten. The new prisons would over-flow, to be followed with a cry to build more, more, absorbing the life blood of the downtrodden. And still the deceptive cry for state education as the standard for decent human survival would once more rear its ugly head. I saw all of this, and was ready for the struggle.

In 1971, I was once more shipped to Angola. That same year, Albert Woodfox, Herman Wallace, and Ronald Ailsworth (among others who had affiliated themselves with the struggle and the Black Panthers) would also enter the prison. Arriving at Angola, I immediately noticed a mood change. There was a new psyche among the prisoners: not the subdued and broken spirit I saw in years past, but one of defiance, of people standing up. The mood in the streets had caught up with the men in prisons, and I knew it was due mainly to the presence of Albert, Herman, and Ron, and their work in spreading the message of the Black Panther Party. They began teaching unity amongst the inmates, establishing the only recognized prison chapter of the Black Panther Party in the nation. Shortly thereafter, Ron was transferred to a federal facility but Albert Woodfox and Herman Wallace were slated to pay dearly for their organizing skills.

Upon my return I found the place in an uproar. Mass lockups and severe repression by prison officials, especially of those quartered in the main prison, were the order of the day. A young prison guard named Brent Miller had been found slain in one of the dormitories and though I had not even been in Angola at the time of the guard's death, I did not escape the unchecked reprisals by the keepers upon the kept. Along with three other brothers, I was taken from the Admitting Unit and sent to the main prison dungeon. The only reason given was that we "wanted to play lawyer for another inmate." In the dungeon, I witnessed even more severe repression. Prisoners who had been scooped up for "investigation" (into the death of the officer) were made to run the gauntlet past guards wielding bats and clubs. They were stripped of all clothing, their heads were shaved, and they were kept in bare, empty cells. White prisoners were spared this humiliation. None were beaten, placed into lockdown, or even investigated in the guard's death. The beatings and intimidation of Black prisoners went on for days. The prison was closed down and visits were suspended. This made it much easier for prison officials to run amok, unchecked.

After about ten days, my three comrades and I were brought to disciplinary court and found guilty of "wanting to play lawyer for another inmate." We were then sentenced to the infamous "Red Hat," where we faced starvation and the threat of death. The Red Hat was the old death house where the electric chair was kept. At this time, it was used to house prisoners the administration wanted to punish. Its cells were about three feet wide by seven feet or so in length, with a slab of concrete for a bed, a naked toilet bowl and a sink that was usually inoperative. Meals, if one were to call them meals, were served in a small bowl. Breakfast was a dab of oatmeal and perhaps one slice of bread, or sometimes a dab of grits in lieu of the oatmeal. Lunch and dinner, served in the same bowl, was boiled greens or carrots with one slice of bread. The Red Hat, at that time, still threatened death, not by electrocution, but by starvation. They closed it down in 1972.

News had already traveled through the prison's grapevine that prison officials (after days of investigation, brutality, and intimidation) had selected four men and charged them with the death of Miller: Albert Woodfox, Herman Wallace, Gilbert Montegut, and Chester Jackson.

In late May 1972, after being transported from the Red Hat back to the Admitting Unit, I was brought before the prison classification board. As I was ushered into the room, I saw a number of ranking officials that I knew. One of them, Hilton Butler, gave me a contemptuous look and said, "Y'all know my vote," then left the room. I was still under investigation for the death of Miller although I had never met the guard, never been in general population where I could have had the opportunity to meet him, and had not even been in Angola prison at the time of his death. Without further ado, I was classified to CCR or closed cell restriction for this reason, a classification I would keep for the next twenty-nine years. They initially sent me to C-tier, then later to D-tier. Woodfox and Herman were initially on B-tier, known at the time as the "Panther Tier."

Sometime in 1973, an official came to D-tier and asked if there was anyone who wanted to volunteer to go to B-tier, that a cell was needed on D. Not knowing all of the particulars, and seizing on the opportunity to be close to Albert and Herman, I volunteered. Once off the tier, I learned of the particulars. The officials meant to separate Herman and Albert from the men of B-tier, figuring to break up the "Panther Tier." The men on B-tier were unaware of this, and I told them what was intended. We knew what was coming, and we made preparations to resist. After a nearly all-night battle against sticks, bats, tear gas, and other more potent weapons — all wielded by the keepers — the separation was made. Wallace went to A-tier, and Woodfox to D-tier, to the very cell that I had volunteered to vacate.

During this time, the men charged in the death of the prison guard were in and out of court. Subsequently, they received a change of venue. Albert Woodfox went to trial separately, and on the testimony of a prison snitch, Hezekiah Brown, was found guilty. There was no evidence whatsoever linking him (or the other men charged) to the crime, save the testimony of the snitch, who, after coercion and promises, fingered the men. Woodfox later received a second trial, based on the fact that the jury that tried him was all white. In this second trial, the jury's foreperson stated that she had found him guilty because he had divulged the information that he had passed a lie detector test. That is so strange! Without any doubt, had Woodfox failed a polygraph test, this same juror would have used this failure (and surely the prosecution would have made it known to the jurors) as evidence to convict him.

As I stated, Hezekiah Brown was a well-known prison snitch. As a former inmate guard, he had no morals. It was easy for him to succumb to the temptation of promises. Brown was promised that he would live in an area by himself, separated from the other prisoners, and be able to come and go as he pleased. He was also promised (and records show that he received) a carton of cigarettes a week. Despite the fact that he had a life sentence without the possibility of parole, Hezekiah Brown was given clemency and released sometime during the eighties. He is reported to have left the prison with nearly a thousand dollars in cash. Hezekiah Brown is now unfortunately deceased, of natural causes.

Herman Wallace and Gilbert Montegut (and allegedly, Chester Jackson) were to be tried jointly, but only Montegut and Wallace were actually tried. Montegut (with the jury hearing the same evidence that convicted Woodfox) was acquitted. Herman Wallace was found guilty. Chester Jackson did not go to trial that day. Instead, he was given a reduced manslaughter charge. The reason for this magnanimity is simple. Chester Jackson (now deceased) was a snitch who, at the urging of prison officials, elected to supply them with corroborating evidence implicating Wallace in the killing. That both Wallace and Woodfox were (and are) innocent is without doubt. Their convictions were a clear act of retribution by prison officials because of their activism, and the need to find scapegoats.

While there was no forensic evidence linking Woodfox or Wallace to the crime, there was evidence that pointed to other sources. According to the trial testimony of Herbert "Professor" Williams, Sr., an orderly whose responsibility was to keep the catwalk clean, the only person he saw on the morning of the killing in the vicinity was a "white boy." This evidence was never pursued by either the state or the defense. The other bit of "evidence" that ran through the prison grapevine was that Miller (the deceased) was killed by one of his own. The infighting that was taking place among prison officials at the time lends credibility to this theory. During this period, Governor Edwin Edwards appointed Elayn Hunt as Corrections Head. Her mission was to "clean up the prison, and bring it into the twenty-first century." To that end, C. Murray Henderson was appointed warden.

Coming from another state, Henderson was seen as an intruder and an outsider by some, who felt that their long tenure on "The Farm" should have qualified them to continue to run the place. This resentment was exacerbated when Henderson brought in his own people. Angriest of all was Hayden Dees, who felt he should have been head warden, not Henderson. It is rumored that Dees — obsessively ambitious, and bitter with resentment — did the unthinkable and ordered the "hit" on Miller (the deceased). If true, Dees, being the racist that he was, would never have sent a Black prisoner to murder a white prison guard.

If all of the above rumors were correct, then it all lends credibility to Herbert "Professor" Williams's trial testimony — that on the morning of the murder, the only person he saw was a "white boy."

CHAPTER 22

AS OF THIS WRITING, HERMAN WALLACE and Albert Woodfox have been held in solitary confinement for more than thirty years. To be held guilty of a crime that one hasn't committed — with exculpatory evidence to prove innocence, evidence that has been willfully overlooked by the courts — is an act of terrorism. But what is even more terrifying is that unless there is an intervention by a court showing integrity, Albert and Herman will have to spend the remainder of their lives in prison, in solitary confinement for a crime neither committed. "Justice delayed is justice denied" and I agree. However, suffice it to say that justice delayed is equal to terrorism, especially in this case. Solitary confinement is terrifying, especially if you are innocent of the charges that put you there. It evokes a lot of emotion. For me, being in prison in solitary confinement was terrible; it was a nightmare. My soul still cries from all that I witnessed and endured. It mourns continuously. Through the course of my confinement, I saw men so desperate that they ripped prison doors apart, and both starved and mutilated themselves. It takes every scrap of humanity to stay focused and sane in that environment. I should be anything but what I am today; sometimes the spirit is stronger than the circumstances.

At some point, we are going to have to call prison exactly what it is: a perpetuation of slavery. The 13th Amendment did not abolish slavery. It reconstituted slavery instead, by putting it on another plane, the prison plane. The 13th Amendment says "neither slavery nor involuntary servitude shall exist on these shores except for persons duly convicted of a crime." But how many have been legally convicted of a crime even though they were innocent? At one point, I mistakenly believed that legality and morality were synonymous, that everything judged legal was also wholly and morally correct. Through hard experience, I learned that this is not true.

The Black Panther Party's slogan "power to the people" centered around the concept that power actually does belong to the people. But the people have relinquished that power to a small faction of people called politicians, and in relinquishing power they have left themselves at the mercy of ever-changing restrictions defined as laws. Many of these laws deemed legal are in no way moral. In reality, we are empowered en masse to direct or redirect our own course. In redirecting our own course, one of the main focuses must be the prison system and how it is connected to slavery.

So let's call prisons exactly what they are: an extenuation of slavery. And we must let the politicians know that we know this. Mumia Abu-Jamal is in prison because slavery was never abolished. Jalil Alamin, formerly Rap Brown; the San Francisco 8, the remaining two of the Angola 3, Herman Wallace and Albert Woodfox; Leonard Peltier; the Jena 6 . . . we could go on naming people, all political victims of a legal system that is in fact immoral. It is a system like this that allows a district attorney, Read Walters, to say to Jena youth Mychael Bell with impunity that "with a stroke of a pen, I can take your life away." It is a system like this that gives district attorneys, defense lawyers, judges, legislators, politicians a vested interest in passing the laws, regulations, decisions, and judgments that keep people in prison. Justice cannot exist when the people charged with defending the rights of people are invested in their incarceration.

During my twenty-nine years of solitary (and the two prior years in parish prison), I lived out the conclusion that the Black Panther Party's assessment of America, as it related to Blacks and other minorities, was correct. Without the Party's appraisal, and my total acceptance of this appraisal, I could not have survived intact those twenty-nine years. I had been given a truth to live by, a truth to cling to. And despite the internal friction among the Party's leaders and cadres (orchestrated by the FBI and CIA), and in spite of the eventual elimination of the Party as an organization by these same forces, this truth has sustained me. I made a vow to myself that no matter what, I would do my best to live out this truth, even in solitary confinement. I told myself that no matter where one resided in America — whether in minimum custody (society) or maximum security custody (prison) — the struggle must continue.

CCR or Closed Cell Restriction (when it was located at the front gate of the prison) was a unit that also housed death row prisoners. The entire unit had seven tiers; each tier (save one) had fifteen single man cells. We were kept in cells twenty-three hours a day, seven days a week. For years, we were denied any yard time. The one hour we were out of our cells was used for showering. Each morning the officer on duty, standing outside of the tier by the control box, would open all the cell doors. When the doors opened, the men wanting to shower would file out of their cells into the hallways. This was the practice until 1974.

On the morning of June 10, 1973, I was still on B-tier. It was on that date that one prisoner, with the intention of knifing another prisoner, but not realizing that his intended victim also had a knife, was killed. Ordinarily, the incident would have gone into the prison books as being a clear case of self defense. But that didn't happen. Instead, officials at the prison issued a "blanket indictment" against all the men who were out of their cells that morning — eleven of us. A short time later, this blanket indictment was dropped against nine of those originally charged. The remaining two men — Grady Brewer and myself — were officially indicted by a Grand Jury on charges of murder.

Neither Grady nor I were actually disturbed by this turn of events, and we both were eager to go to trial. Grady felt that no reasonable jury would find him guilty of murder, for he had acted in self-defense. I was eager because I had nothing to do with the incident, and was sure that I could prove it to a jury.

The trial was held in rural St. Francisville, about 20 miles south of the prison. The town's residents, especially the whites, didn't take too kindly to prisoners confined at Angola, in spite of the fact that many of them (the males, that is) worked at the prison. Those who didn't knew someone who did and it was from this linkage that jury pools were created.

Grady Brewer and I were to be tried jointly and the trial began on October 10, 1973. Our appointed council made it known to the judge that he hadn't enough time to prepare, and asked for an extension, which the court promptly refused. At that point, Grady and I got into the act. We tried to convince the court that we needed more time; the judge was adamant. Some more words were passed, resulting in our having to stand trial with our hands cuffed behind our backs, in shackles, with tape over our mouths. For two days, we sat in court, gagged and in chains, and watched the jury being picked to try us.

The state began its case by entering nine knives allegedly found near or in close proximity to the body, into evidence. This was despite the fact that the coroner's report stated that "all of the wounds appear to have been made with the same weapon." In the subsequent testimony, none of the officers who were on duty that morning implicated me as a participant. No fingerprints of mine were found on any of the knives. Nevertheless, the state produced two surprise witnesses in the persons of two of the inmates who were out of their cells that morning. Both inmates — with tailored testimonies — testified that I had participated in the murder, which in fact was a self-defense killing. Both their testimonies were riddled with inconsistencies, and they both lied about the events of that morning. One was in fact caught in a lie on the witness stand. Nevertheless, on the testimony of the other inmate — who had not witnessed the incident — Grady and I were found guilty as charged.

In 1974, the Louisiana State Supreme Court reversed my life sentence and ordered a new trial. The reversal was not based on my innocence, but because the trial judge had abused his power by having me bound and gagged. In 1975, a second trial began and on the same frail evidence as before, I was found guilty a second time.

Some time during 1975, I found myself back on D-tier, right next door to Woodfox. We resumed our political education classes, holding discussions and teaching those who couldn't read or write to do so. Our efforts did not go unnoticed by our keepers: we were constantly being harassed, and worse. Once, an inmate "trusty" approached Woodfox, saying: "I know y'all wants to escape, so I'm gon' help y'all." He pulled out a fully loaded .32 revolver and handed it to Woodfox. After taking the pistol and examining it, Woodfox handed it back to him, telling him, "Thank you, but I'll find another way." Woodfox had seen that the firing pin had been filed to the nub. It was obviously a set-up. Not long after that incident, a group of security officers went to Woodfox's cell to "shake him down," or search his belongings. After handcuffing Albert and placing him in the hallway, the search began. I heard one of the officers yell, "Bingo, look what I found." The officer came out of the cell holding a small pouch containing gunpowder. As a result, Woodfox spent quite a few days in isolation. There is no doubt that the item "found" in Woodfox's cell was planted. It was a set-up that gave them the excuse needed to justify a major shakedown and to literally "tear up" our cells.

The fact that we were constantly harassed and targeted by prison officials did not deter us in our efforts to change our conditions. We clearly understood the extreme limitations the keepers placed on us, but we were determined to eliminate some of those unnecessary restrictions. Therefore, we continued to set examples of resistance, examples that other prisoners in other areas could identify with.

During the years from 1974 to 1978, we experienced some successes from our willingness to struggle; prisoners throughout the prison (and even in some parish jails) began hearing of our accomplishments in CCR, especially in D-tier. Quite a few prisoners wanted to become part of us and do what we were doing. Some did.

Each tier consisted of fifteen cells, six feet by nine feet, and the doors were barred. A long walkway connected them, with the shower at the front of each tier. The one hour a day that we were released from our cells we spent taking our shower, and then in that walkway. That was how we talked, passed papers, educated each other, and coordinated our actions.

One of our successes was the elimination of a long-standing practice of feeding us. At mealtime our food was taken from a cart and placed on the floor in front of each cell. The prisoner then had to reach down and retrieve the tray by sliding it under a filthy door, losing some of the food in the process. Almost every cellblock was fed in this dehumanizing manner. Sensing how humiliating this practice was, we began to feel unclean, and angry with ourselves for having allowed ourselves to participate in our own victimization. After discussing the matter amongst ourselves, we decided that we would try to negotiate with the keepers. The prison administration told us that this was non-negotiable, that "We always fed that way, and it will continue." Plan B was simple enough: we went on a hunger strike. After many days of hunger, a representative of the warden came to us, telling us that if we would discontinue the hunger strike, the warden would at some point honor our request, by cutting holes in the bars large enough for a tray to pass through. Knowing that "at some point" meant many months, we continued with our hunger strike. We fasted for more than thirty days, and sometime after that point, the representative came back. After talking and wrangling a bit, it was agreed that until the holes were cut in the bars, we would be allowed to tie a sling made of cloth to our bars that would hold the trays. For nearly eighteen months we ate from slings, standing up at the bars. After that, the prison began cutting holes in every area. However, it must be noted that in a final gesture of utter contempt for us, the prison administration made sure that D-tier was the very last tier to be corrected.

We were also successful in curtailing another routine, a dehumanizing, long-standing practice by the prison — the unnecessary and random rectal searches. During a strip search, we were required to undergo a visual anal search. We told ourselves that this practice served no penological purpose whatsoever; wherever we went, we were chained up, hand and feet. Coming to a consensus conclusion that this practice was a carryover from slavery (before being sold, the slave had to be stripped and subjected to anal examination), and after months of appealing to our keepers, we decided to take a bold step: we would simply refuse a voluntary anal search. We would not be willing participants in our own degradation. We knew that there would be consequences, but we were more than willing to make the necessary sacrifices. We knew it could even mean death. We also knew that we, as a unit, would be disunited — separated by our keepers. With this in mind, addresses and telephone numbers of relatives outside were exchanged.

After having tried for months to get the keepers to discontinue this dehumanizing practice, we began refusing. They came, as we knew they would. My turn came around. I was taken from my cell, handcuffed and shackled, to a remote office room where prison guards lined the walls, some carrying bats, other brandishing billy clubs and other assault weapons. I was ordered to strip, after their removal of the chains. I did. Mind you, we were not refusing the strip search, only the visual anal examination. I was then told to turn around and bend over. Naturally, I refused. I then readied myself for the ensuing onslaught which had to come. It came. We fought. Finally, I was subdued by sheer force of numbers. This was 1977.

After being taken to the prison hospital to have my many bruises examined, I was removed immediately to Camp J, the newly built punishment camp, and charged with multiple counts of assaulting officers (charges were later dropped). The irony is, no anal examination occurred that night.

Meanwhile, Woodfox, who remained at CCR, managed to contact some of my relatives who called the prison inquiring about my health and well-being. This gesture saved me from additional injuries, and perhaps death as well. Someone on the outside had shown concern.

Camp J was purely punitive. The practice of feeding prisoners was identical to the way we had been fed in CCR, prior to our protests. I was told that I would not be allowed to even put a sling on the bars as I done at CCR. Thus, I began a one-man protest.

After making my point, by making clear to my keepers that I would absolutely not "eat off the floor," I ceased my hunger strike. I talked to the inmate orderlies, explaining to them why I wouldn't touch a tray they had set on the floor. Most understood, and would put the tray into my outstretched hand. I would then take the food I intended to eat from the tray folding the paper plate and pulling it through the bars. I always kept a cleaning rag to wipe up any spillage. I did this for better than two years. It wasn't until after I was sent back to CCR that the keepers cut holes in the bars at Camp J.

Prior to our having decided to resist the dehumanizing anal searches, we had talked about contacting an attorney to assist us in a civil suit. And during intervals, when Woodfox wasn't in the dungeon for refusing the search, he contacted NOLAC, or New Orleans Legal Assistance. Recognizing the merits of the case, they decided to assist us in the case, representing us jointly. The suit (*Woodfox, et al vs. Phelps, et al*) was filed in the Nineteenth District Court, and less than a year later the court issued a ruling, outlawing "routine anal searches." Sulking, the prison officials reluctantly ceased this practice. Presently, anal searches are conducted only when "warranted," whatever that means.

I was at Camp J for more than two years, and the Struggle continued. Besides the inhumane practices, there were far greater atrocities. The physical and psychological torture of prisoners was unchecked. I was told by officials at the camp that what they were doing was condoned by persons in high places. I believed them; how else, unless it was "condoned by persons in high places," could it have gone on for so long? Prisoners had no access to personal phone calls and could not inform their relatives as to what was happening to them. There was no access to law books to properly challenge the practices. We were in cells twenty-three hours a day, at times twenty-four. Yard privileges were non-existent. Death by alleged suicide emerged around the same time as Camp J came into existence. A psychiatric unit was built, mostly for victims of Camp J's atrocities. After my stint at Camp J, I was returned to CCR. This was around November 1979.

In early 1981, I was once more residing on the tier with Woodfox. We shared the same tier until 1996, when — after having his original conviction and sentence of fifty years overturned — he was immediately retried for the alleged murder of prison guard Brent Miller. As in the first trial, Woodfox was convicted and given a life sentence. He was returned to the custody of the Department of Corrections, back to CCR and his former solitary confinement status within the prison. His struggle continues . . .

CHAPTER 23

IN 1987, THE LONE INMATE ON WHOSE testimony my conviction rested made it known to me through another inmate that he "wanted to set the record straight." He wanted to make it known publicly that he had lied throughout my trials, that he had not witnessed the incident on the morning that it had happened. This inmate later provided me with an affidavit to this effect. Shortly thereafter, I received a notarized statement from the other inmate who had testified against me during the first trial but had failed to appear during the second trial. In 1988, armed with these affidavits, I optimistically began post-conviction appeals, seeking relief based upon my actual innocence. But just claiming actual innocence was not enough. I also knew that I had to convince a reviewing court that my trial was unfair. So I included other claims: that I was denied the right to cross-examine the witnesses against me; that my council was ineffective; and that women were systematically excluded from the Grand Jury that had indicted me.

After many years of denials in the state courts, and still going *pro se*, I filed a petition for a writ of habeas corpus in the federal court, where a lone federal magistrate denied the petition. Undaunted, I appealed his decision to a panel of three judges. Constrained by a previous ruling, that panel granted relief, ordering a new trial. But in the doublespeak jargon that the courts are noted for, the panel suggested a full court review of its own decision, which automatically stayed the mandate. After a full court hearing consisting of more than a dozen judges, the panel's decision granting me a new trial was reversed. This was in 1993.

As required by law, the federal court at the appellate level had appointed me counsel to argue the case. His name was Christopher A. Aberle. He had argued the case before the panel, and proceeded to argue the case before the full court. After the full court reversed the panel's order, Aberle filed a writ of *certiorari* to the U.S. Supreme Court. In turn, the high court refused to entertain the petition. This was in 1995.

During this time, I was pondering ways to return to the federal court. This despite my already having had my "one bite at the apple." I was feeling cheated because the federal court, while having granted (and then denied) me a new trial on procedural grounds, had merely brushed aside all evidence pertinent to my actual innocence. With that in mind, I cast my focus on another case, *Kuhlmann vs. Wilson*, 106 S. Ct. 2616 (1986). The United States Supreme Court stated in *Kuhlmann vs. Wilson*, in part, "That claims raised in an earlier federal habeas petition that was resolved adversely to a petitioner may be entertained in a subsequent federal habeas petition if the 'ends of justice' would be served." That ruling alone afforded me "another bite at the apple" and a subsequent ruling, in *Schlup vs. Delo*, 513 U.S. 222 (1995), strengthened and expanded upon the "ends of justice" doctrine. While I was studying, pondering and analyzing the legal ramifications of the two cases — knowing that I would eventually be going back to the courts — I received an unexpected, hand-written letter from my former lawyer, Christopher A. Aberle. In short, and in gist, the letter simply stated: "I'd be willing to represent you (*pro bono*) in a hearing for clemency on the pardon board, if you are interested." Accompanying the letter was the standard form used for a clemency request. Feeling that this was a useless gesture, I nevertheless filled out the form and sent it in. The request to seek clemency was denied. Reason: I was not granted a hearing because I had not served enough time. At this time, I was into my twenty-sixth year of confinement.

Since my former attorney, Chris Aberle, had extended an offer to aid me beyond the clemency process, I made my plans known to him that I was thinking about returning to the courts. He thought it was an excellent idea, and he was eager to help. Like myself, Chris felt that the courts (both state and federal) had dealt unfairly with my original claims. Communicating via mail, we discussed the possibilities of re-raising those same issues, but elaborating more on the issue of ineffective assistance of counsel. Chris would do the work, arguing and framing the petition and I would submit the writ to the court, *pro se*.

It didn't take long for the state courts to deny me. However, once we reentered the federal court, it took more than two years for the magistrate to make a ruling. He did so after being ordered to do so by the then Senior Judge Parker as a result of a federal *mandamus* filed by Chris.

The filing of a *mandamus* in a federal court is very rare and unusual; it is rarely done. Defense counsel tends to shy away from having to file such a petition. They don't want to piss off a federal judge or magistrate who might be sitting on a petition with the thought of being favorable to their client. However, in my case, for a judge to sit on the writ for more than two years could only mean one thing: that judge was looking for a reason to deny the petition. Chris knew this, and I knew this also. Plus, this same judge was the very same individual who had denied me some years earlier, going against the precedent that had been set by the federal appellate court. As anticipated, he denied the petition. But in his haste to deny the petition, the judge went on to say that under *Schlup vs. Delo* (the precedent that I had cited) it appeared that I had met one of the two required standards in *Schlup*; the one showing that I was probably innocent. Thus, though the petition was denied, the ruling gave me hope. I had finally gotten a court to acknowledge the innocence factor. This was in 1998, twenty-five years after I was framed and convicted by prison officials utilizing the false testimony of inmates and twelve years after those same inmates had recanted their testimonies, exposing the lies and frame-ups.

It was also in 1998 that I was called by court order to appear as a character witness for Albert Woodfox, who had won a new trial to be held in Amite, Louisiana. I was there for approximately two weeks, and the things that I witnessed there propelled me to recommit myself to the struggle.

The jail, recently built, was designed to house about 650 prisoners on a temporary basis. It actually held about 1,200. Over 90 percent of the inmates were Black, and the average age was twenty-two. Most of those prisoners were kept in detention for years instead of being sent to Angola or another state prison. The Louisiana legislature had decided to allow local detention centers and parish jails, entirely unequipped to handle large numbers of inmates for long periods of time, to serve as penitentiaries. This allowed federal and state funds to be diverted to local sheriffs and other municipal authorities charged with enforcing the law. But how can the law be fairly enforced when those who enforce it receive money for imprisoning people? When a parish receives extra funding for every person it locks up in the local jail, then their only incentive is to lock more people up. This is but one example of the legislation and legal maneuvering done to perpetuate slavery. What was taking place in Amite was surely being replicated in each of Louisiana's sixty-four parishes.

I KNEW FROM WHAT I SAW AT AMITE THAT the Struggle continued. At this point, while I felt a bit more hopeful about my own case, I knew that the real battle for my freedom from prison still had to be waged. I had another major hurdle to cross: I had to convince a court that during my trial, a major constitutional violation had occurred.

Chris went to work on a new habeas corpus petition. When it was finished, it was a work of art. In the ensuing months, while we waited for a decision, Chris, convinced that the habeas would probably be denied, wrote a letter which appears here in its entirety:

> April 30, 1999
> Charles A. Shropshire
> District Attorney
> 20th Judicial District Court
> 499 Royal Street
> St. Francisville, LA 70775
>
> Dear Mr. Shropshire:
>
> I write wondering whether you wouldn't mind reopening the 25-year-old murder case of State v. Robert King Wilkerson and then dismissing the case, so that Mr. Wilkerson can be released from Angola.
>
> I suspect that you have never had such a request, at least not from an attorney, but before you ball up this

letter and throw it away, I respectfully request your indulgence for the time it will take to get to the end of this letter.

Let me begin by noting that I have never before made such a request and I don't anticipate having the opportunity to do so again. This case, however, is unusual. I was appointed to represent Mr. Wilkerson by the U.S. Fifth Circuit back in the early 1990s in his appeal from the federal district court's denial of habeas corpus relief. Not only was Mr. Wilkerson my first appointed case, he was my first client. Prior to that, I had been a staff attorney in the U.S. Court of Appeals for four years, where I screened over 400 criminal and habeas appeals. Since that appointment, I have represented convicted criminal defendants in about 150 appeals, most of them through my association with the Louisiana Appellate Project, an entity with which I am sure you are familiar.

Of course, as is the nature of criminal appellate defense, I have lost the vast majority of my cases. While a few of those were mildly troubling, I know that justice was achieved in most of those cases. No matter how hard I try, however, I cannot say the same thing for my first case.

Mr. Wilkerson is an African-American inmate, who was accused of murdering a fellow inmate. He had been tried twice in the mid 1970s for this crime and was represented both times by Mr. Leslie Ligon. The first time, he was tried with a codefendant. Because the codefendant was unruly, the trial court ordered that both defendants be bound and gagged throughout the trial. The conviction was reversed as to Mr. Wilkerson because he had done nothing to justify his being presented to the jury in this fashion. Nevertheless, at the second trial, Mr. Wilkerson was bound, but not gagged, and he wore a prison suit. He was also surrounded by a small army of armed law enforcement personnel.

The evidence in the case (the second trial) consisted *solely* of the testimony of a fellow inmate. Although all of the inmates on the tier witnessed the crime, only this witness testified against Mr. Wilkerson. Every inmate on the tier was charged with this murder except this witness, and, in exchange for testifying, he was moved out of his maximum security surroundings and given trustee status. Unfortunately for Mr. Wilkerson, the trial judge would not permit Mr. Ligon to cross examine this witness about his receiving a prison transfer in connection with his request to testify.

The case looked very good to me. I challenged his conviction on the grounds that he and his witnesses should not have been presented to the jury in shackles, prison garb, and surrounded by so many law enforcement officers. I also argued that the limitation on cross examination of the State's eyewitness regarding his motivation to lie constituted a grossly serious violation of Mr. Wilkerson's right to present a defense. Finally, I included a purely academic argument relating to the fact that there were no women on the grand jury venire. After all, I was appointed because of that issue. Mr. Wilkerson won in the Fifth Circuit on the grand jury argument, and the other issues were given nominal mention and then rejected. It soon became clear to me that the whole reason that I was appointed and that Mr. Wilkerson won the grand jury issue was so that the court could take the case en banc and overrule one of its pesky prior opinions that it felt was a thorn in its side. Mr. Jesse Means can tell you all about it. He was my opposing counsel. Unfortunately, given the court of appeals' motivations, Mr. Wilkerson's truly meaningful claims were brushed aside, and ultimately, I regret raising the grand jury issue on appeal.

It is now several years later, and I still represent Mr. Wilkerson. It turns out that three witness have executed affidavits completely exonerating Mr. Wilkerson. One affidavit comes from Mr. Wilkerson's codefendant. He swears that he, and only he, committed the murder. Another affidavit was executed by an inmate on the tier who testified against Mr. Wilkerson at the first trial. He now swears that prison officials coerced him into testifying, that he was standing next to Mr. Wilkerson during the commission of the crime, and that Mr. Wilkerson had nothing to do with it. The third witness turns out to be the sole eyewitness who testified at Mr. Wilkerson's second trial. He too swears that he lied out of coercion by prison officials, and that Mr. Wilkerson is innocent. Additionally, a review of the testimony of prison guard John Baugh given only at the first trial, corroborates two of the affiants' claims that they had previously lied.

A carefully detailed discussion of the evidence from both trials, the excluded evidence regarding the sole eyewitness's change in custody status, and the newly acquired affidavits are provided on pages 11-23 of the enclosed brief which is a copy of the brief in the appeal that is currently pending in the court of appeals. The appeal is from the district court's denial of Mr. Wilkerson's second habeas petition I filed for him a few years ago. Last month, Mr. Means was contacted by the court of appeals to provide copies of the state court records to aid in the court's review of that appeal.

Notwithstanding my strong belief that Mr. Wilkerson *should* win that appeal, I know he won't. Habeas petitioners almost never win in the fifth circuit, regardless of the merits of their claims, and I surely don't expect the court to be too receptive to claims they have already addressed in a prior petition. I know that if Mr. Wilkerson had not been a convicted robber at the time of the murder and if his victim had not been a convicted African American, then he would have stood a better chance on his long road through the criminal justice system. If, in addition, Mr. Wilkerson had been given the death penalty, there would have been an international outcry if the courts tossed him aside as they have done so far. But, alas, Mr. Wilkerson was already a criminal at the time of the murder, and his alleged victim was likewise a convicted African-American prisoner. In addition this shackled, Black criminal was tried by a predominantly white male jury in the 1970s in rural Louisiana. Mr. Wilkerson never stood a chance then, and now nobody much cares if an injustice may have occurred in this case. I think you would agree with me, however, that neither the defendant's status nor his victim's status should be factors in determining whether it is OK to convict a man wrongly.

My decision to write to you was inspired by a bit of news I had heard one day about a similar case in some other part of the country. I don't remember where this took place, but like Mr. Wilkerson's case, the evidence in that case, including new evidence, cast considerable doubt over the validity of the conviction. As with Mr. Wilkerson, this defendant's venture into the courts for redress was unavailing, due mostly to the procedural quagmires a habeas litigant faces. Then his attorney wrote a letter to the district attorney who agreed to reopen the case and dismiss the charges. In my years as a lawyer, I had never heard of such a thing, though in retrospect it makes perfect sense. After all, your job is not merely to put people in jail but to see that justice is done as well.

Accordingly, I write to ask you, humbly and respectfully, to review the enclosed brief and affidavits. Additionally, I can supply you with the two trial

> transcripts if you so request. After reading what I have written and verifying its accuracy, I suggest you will agree with me that the chances are pretty slim that Mr. Wilkerson deserves to be serving time for murder. If I am right and you do indeed feel that way, I would urge you to do what is in your power to give this man his freedom while he still has some good years left. Mr. Wilkerson is a very intelligent man and has become quite learned in his years at Angola. Lord knows, we need the bed space at Angola for the truly bad guys.
>
> If you review this case and don't conclude that an injustice has been done, I apologize for taking your time. But PLEASE do not come to that conclusion before reading the enclosed materials. You are the end of the road for Mr. Wilkerson's decade-long attempt at being a free man.
>
> Your time and attention are greatly appreciated.
> Very truly yours,
> Christopher A. Aberle

When a single judge on the Court of Appeals for the Fifth Circuit denied probable cause, in 2000, Chris filed for a re-hearing. Then an unusual thing happened: the first judge suddenly revoked his own order of denial and ordered a hearing to be conducted before a three-judge panel to deal with the merits of my case. Additionally, the order stated that Chris, who had been acting *pro bono* (for free) on my behalf for many years, was appointed by the court to represent me in any future proceedings: this meant he would be getting paid to represent me!

In 1998, when Albert "Cinque" Woodfox was retried and convicted, a small grassroots movement consisting mostly of anarchists (thanks to Malik Rahim, a.k.a. Donald Guyton, one of the Panthers arrested in the first raid by New Orleans Police) had heard about the case and had come on board. This group showed its support by appearing at hearings and at the trial of Woodfox, held in the small town of Amite, Louisiana, home of the family of the security guard he was accused of slaying. During this time, support centered around Albert and Herman "Hooks" Wallace, and it was the "Committee to support/free the Angola Two." Later, however, with the insistence of Woodfox, it became the Committee to Free the Angola 3, myself included. Still later, it became the National Coalition to Free the Angola 3.

By the time I was to have my hearing, efforts by the national coalition had intensified. Marion H. Brown, a former Tulane student and Panther, along with Althea Francois, another former Panther, had come on board. It was their grassroots organizing, getting information into the Black community, that paid off and set the catalyst for the national and international attention that the Angola 3 now get. There were also others who helped. Former journalist Leslie George of WBAI radio in New York City broadcast interviews that were heard by thousands. Marina Drummer of Berkeley, California, was dubbed "The Navigator" because she, from long distance, navigated the course of the Angola 3 like none other. She wrote to anybody she thought she could interest and influence to get involved. Scott Fleming, then a law student (since become a lawyer, defending Herman and Albert) also did outreach to others, seeking aid for the Angola 3. Rose Braz, Gail Shaw, Bill Jennings (of "It's About Time"), Richard Becker, Louis (Bato) Talementez, and so many many others who time and space will not allow me to name, all came on board in an unselfish effort to support the Angola 3.

My hearing in federal court before a three-judge panel, was held in the year 2000. I was not allowed to attend. The courtroom, I was told, was packed with supporters: college, high school, and elementary students; community activists; and, of course, former members of the Black Panther Party, including Marion Brown and Althea Francois. There were several other cases heard by that panel that day, but I was told that when my lawyers concluded their arguments, the courtroom immediately emptied. This was a signal to the judges that the courtroom had only been filled because of my case.

During the first week of February 2001, I was told by security that I needed to call my lawyer. The news from Chris was stunning! He had been advised by the District Attorney's office, in St. Francisville, LA, that if I elected to plead guilty to a lesser charge of accessory-after-the-fact, I could be home within a week! While I didn't wish to admit guilt or any culpability, accessory-after-the-fact was no biggie. Shit, everyone on the tier at the time of the incident knew that a death had occurred. The hearing was set for the morning of February 8, 2001, in the Twenty-First judicial district court, St. Francisville, LA.

A day before the scheduled hearing, I was again told that I needed to call my attorney. His message was that the District Attorney, fearing a civil suit, had upped the ante. As a measure of security (to forestall possible lawsuits) the state now wanted me to plead guilty to the reduced charge of manslaughter. I had no intention of suing the state; however, I also had no intention of pleading guilty to manslaughter, despite the fact that I was being urged to by my two comrades and other supporters. Perhaps knowing this, and still fearing a lawsuit, the State dropped the ante again. Chris was told by the District Attorney's office that I would go free if I would plead guilty to the lesser charge of "conspiracy to commit murder."

On the date of the hearing, the courtroom was packed with supporters from several states. Most of them did not know of these negotiations. All they knew was that I would probably be coming home soon. Their efforts on behalf of the Angola 3, and on behalf of me specifically, were to be rewarded. Many, including my two comrades, felt that my release could somehow impact the ultimate release of Herman and Albert. And so, after serving thirty-one years in prison (twenty-nine in solitary) for crimes I did not commit, I elected to plead guilty to conspiracy to commit murder. In a final gesture of contempt, when the judge asked me to raise my right hand to tell the truth, I threw up my left. The courtroom was packed, and I believe only one person there caught my gesture. It was the District Attorney, who gave me a most peculiar look, but said nothing when our eyes met.

The district court judge computed my sentence to "time served." All of my supporters who had come to the courthouse also came to the front gate of Angola State Prison, awaiting my release. Verna Mae was the only relative among them. I was scheduled to be released on February 9, 2001, at 12:01 a.m., the prison authorities, perhaps eyeing the crowd, decided to not wait. At approximately 4:12 p.m., February 8, 2001, in the midst of a throng of cheering supporters and guys cheering from death row, I walked free at last.

POSTSCRIPT

UPON MY RELEASE FROM PRISON, I MADE the promise that "Even though I was free from Angola, Angola would never be free of me." Since my release, I have traveled north, south, east, and west, speaking at colleges and universities, telling of my plight and that of the rest of the Angola 3 and other political prisoners who are confined in this nation's prisons and of others who have been wrongfully convicted and prosecuted. Also, I've traveled to more than a dozen different countries, some three or more times, telling folks about America and its fabled judicial system, exposing that it is synonymous with the chattel slave system of yesteryear. The only difference is that America has found a way to legalize the enslavement of its citizens through imprisonment, as only America can do!

Again I'll say that legality and morality are opposites in this country. And contrary to what people may believe, the deeper discussion at this time should not just be about the immorality inherent in the American legal system, but rather about the people relinquishing their power. We the people are our own greatest resource. We, not elected officials, are empowered en masse to redirect our own course. And in redirecting our course, one of our main focuses has to be the prison system and how it is linked to the slavery of old.

Whether my release from prison has positively impacted the cases of Albert and Herman remains to be seen. I will continue to champion their cause, as well as that of other prisoners. The National Coalition to Free the Angola 3 (and other political prisoners and political victims), with branches in New Orleans,

Texas, New York, Chicago, and California and with supporters in England, Amsterdam (Holland), Paris, Portugal, Belgium, Germany, and Africa, will not give up the fight. We all know that . . .

The Struggle Continues!
ROBERT HILLARY KING
a.k.a.
ROBERT KING WILKERSON
Freed Member of the Angola 3

EPILOGUE

JUNE 2012

Since my release from Angola State Prison on February 8, 2001, after serving a total of thirty-one years, twenty nine of which were in solitary confinement, my mission has been to campaign both for the release of Herman and Albert and for an end to the cruel and immoral legal system, which tortures and wrongly incarcerates many thousands of Hermans and Alberts.

The campaign to Free the Angola 3 has grown from strength to strength, from the supporters who first came to visit us in Angola and got the word out, through to the culmination of years of work by numerous grassroots activists and progressive social justice organizations such as ACLU, Color of Change, Critical Resistance, CURE, NAACP, Prison Radio, RAE, Safe Streets and many others. The campaign has now reached the attention of U.S. legislators and congresspeople at state and national levels, worldwide opinion-formers, the international media, and large global NGOs such as Amnesty International. They have all come on board calling for justice.

Efforts around the Angola 3 case had a most humble beginning back in 1997, when Colonel Nyati Bolt, recently released from twenty years in Angola, began passing out flyers in San Francisco about Herman and Albert. Bolt ran into transplanted New Orleans resident and activist Malik Rahim, who remembered both Herman and Albert from Orleans Parish Prison in the early 1970s. Rahim couldn't believe that the men were still incarcerated in Angola, and set about organizing a support committee. Simultaneously Scott Fleming, a young law student at

U.C. Berkeley's Boalt Hall, was volunteering at Prison Activist Resource Center in Oakland. The letter from Herman Wallace, who had written to PARC in a desperate attempt to get some legal help for an upcoming hearing for Albert Woodfox, would change his life and the lives of Herman and Albert.

Malik did the outreach and the background work necessary to build a strong support committee. Many of the original members are still involved some fifteen years later, and waves of new supporters have joined the effort since those early days. Scott took on the case while still in law school. With much research and hard work, he prepared the original legal documents that helped reopen the case to further hearings. In the case's early years, there was no legal assistance, no investigative help, and absolutely no media attention. The case has now taken on a momentum and life of its own, creating remarkable connections and undergoing fascinating twists and turns. Robert King's release in 2001 added a new and critical dimension to outreach efforts. Dame Anita Roddick's interest and support evolved after her passing to a dedicated effort by her husband, Gordon, and his circle of friends and acquaintances. The film *In the Land of the Free*, done in Anita's memory by filmmaker Vadim Jean has created worldwide recognition and sympathy.

Artist Rigo 23 has also taken the story of the Angola 3 to the far corners of the world to gain attention and I have gone with him, from meetings with the ANC in South Africa to a world peace congress with Desmond Tutu. My mission has taken me to five continents: most of the states in North America, Brazil and Venezuela in South America, Bali in Asia, South Africa and countries across Europe. I have spoken to thousands of young people, students, governments, NGOs, lawyers, and those involved in the social justice movement. It would be impossible to tell you what has touched me the most, but included here is an account of one of the most memorable to the country of South Africa, struggling with the historical effects of its own kind of racism and apartheid. I travel to talk, to tell the world about America's injustices as I have lived them, and as tens of thousands of others still live them. So it seemed important to also include a transcript of one of these talks, how people react to them and the kind of questions they ask me. The last two pieces in the epilogue are political commentaries that should have been included in the first book, but are here rewritten and updated as, 'What's in a Name (Vulgarizing . . . Vulgarity)', and 'Shaka, or Checks and Balances.'

My focus is always on the case of the Angola 3, but also about human rights and the abuses that take place in the prison system. Herman and Albert's struggle is that of everyone unjustly incarcerated. I have seen how these debates have evolved, shifted and grown in strength over the years. In the eleven years since my release the public discourse on prisons and the criminal justice system has broadened considerably. There is more information available on the racially skewed statistics and the utter disparity in stopping, arresting, sentencing people of color then there ever has been before. Most recently Michelle Alexander's book, *The New Jim Crow*, opened up a critical dialogue on the injustice in this country to a wide new audience. There was little to no discussion back in our early organizing days that dealt with the expansion and abuse of solitary confinement as a means of torture. From those days to the present we have been blessed with a wide new network of support and information from Solitary Watch to special campaigns dealing with solitary through Amnesty, the ACLU, American Friends Service Committee, and others. The UN Special Rapporteur recently released a report on the extended use of solitary in American prisons, declaring it a form of torture.

Tuesday, April 17, 2012, marked 40 years of incarceration in solitary confinement for my two comrades, Albert Woodfox and Herman Wallace. On that day the world stood up against this injustice. Thousands of people from 125 countries were with us in spirit at the State Capitol in Baton Rouge, Louisiana with representatives from Amnesty USA. Other organizations stood by our side including the NAACP, National Action Network, and Congresswoman Patricia Smith, Chair of the Louisiana

Black Caucus. With fellow Angola 3 supporters we handed in a petition of over 65,000 signatures to Governor Jindal demanding Herman and Albert's immediate release from solitary confinement. United we all called for justice. Justice from the torture of solitary confinement. Freedom from wrongful conviction.

Amnesty International USA has joined us in our struggle. "The 40-year isolated incarceration of these two men is scandalous," Everette Harvey Thompson, Southern Office Regional Director, has said. "It pushes the boundaries of cruel, inhuman and degrading treatment, and flies in the face of international standards to which the US is a party. What evidence is there that these men are so dangerous that they must be subjected to these conditions? They have clean disciplinary histories, they are old men and four decades of solitary confinement has left them physically and mentally frail. There is no legitimate penal purpose for keeping these men in solitary. Louisiana authorities must end this inhumanity."[1]

There is no doubt that public pressure coming from members of organizations such as Amnesty International matters. I know that public pressure works and that public opinion matters. I have seen it at work in the courts. I have seen how it can make a difference in the decision making of those in the system with the power to determine a sentence, a verdict or a judgment. I have also seen it at work in the media when they report on the stories that must be told, and further raise awareness of the case and wider issues. But we must not only continue because of these facts, we must continue because the authorities need to know that people are watching them and that they are accountable to us, the people.

Standing on the State Capitol steps on Tuesday 17 April, I felt the power of the people — of 65,000 people and more. All those who have supported the Angola 3 over the years were also with us. We could not be ignored — the media were there and wanted to report on this, organizations stood by our side in support.

1. http://www.amnesty.org/en/news/us-authorities-urged-end-two-men-s-40-year-long-solitary-imprisonment-2012-04-13.

Amnesty's presence was felt. For me the day was bittersweet, bitter with a deep sadness that we were marking this day, but sweet seeing the years of efforts and struggle culminating in this day. The tide is changing and the time for change is now. We have the wind at our back and we need to keep on moving . . .

This is true even though this year we have lost some dear comrades in the struggle who have returned to the ancestors; Geronimo Ji Jaga, Marilyn Buck, and all those in between. We are also mindful of the fact that Mumia has been granted a reprieve from imminent death. However we also need to remind ourselves that life in prison is incremental death. Knowing what I know, and knowing the illegal and inhumane torture that Herman and Albert endure on U.S. soil, I will continue to shine a light on injustice wherever it rears its ugly head. The fight for justice never ends . . . the fight to free Herman and Albert and all political prisoners continues. This is their legacy and this is ours.

All power to the people.
King

WHITHER SOUTH AFRICA: JOURNEY TO THE BELOVED COUNTRY

MARINA DRUMMER

IN SPRING OF 2003, MY FRIEND AND co-conspirator, internationally renowned Madeiran artist Rigo 23 contacted me about a plan he had to take Robert King Wilkerson, the recently released member of the Angola 3, to Africa. Rigo envisioned a journey to Tanzania to meet up with previous political prisoner, Geronimo Ji Jaga Pratt. The plan was that in Tanzania, Robert and Geronimo would climb Mt. Kilimanjaro and then travel on to South Africa where Robert would meet with African National Congress members and perhaps, even, Nelson Mandela. His vision included a filmmaker that would document the entire adventure.

As with everything Rigo does through his cultural and political activism, it was a bold and media-catching notion. At the time, I remember thinking it sounded like a lovely idea, but one that would be far too expensive to implement and also full of complexities and uncertainties. As an administrator and not an artist, I tend to focus on the mundane and doable objectives of organizing and all too frequently, miss the really remarkable things that can be done.

As the months passed, and the trip began to take shape, the vision of what Rigo was doing grew on me. The notion of freed political prisoners climbing the legendary Kilimanjaro and of Robert, released after 29 years in solitary for a crime he did not commit, meeting with the ANC and Mandela provided a much needed image of healing and of hope. Rigo continued organizing and even found a kindred spirit in Marc Chiat of Red Dog Films, who was willing to fund the travel portion of this epic journey.

Now, almost a year later, in hopes of inspiring others it seems fitting, if long

overdue, to share what I've heard from Robert and Rigo about their sojourn. After scurrying around for the right vaccinations and visas and papers, Robert set off to meet Rigo in Portugal on July 14, 2003. Rigo had set up several events in Lisbon. Robert had been to Portugal before and met with activists in the ghettos of Lisbon. By interesting coincidence, the ghettos were filled with immigrants and descendants from Angola. The Louisiana State Penitentiary was named Angola, as most of the slaves in this area were from this African country.

Their first event was the one-year commemoration of the killing of a young man from the Lisbon ghetto, shot dead by local police. This young man had been a local organizer and community leader and the media came out to televise the demonstration to commemorate his murder. Robert spoke with his mother and with other community members and the international solidarity that comes with racism and repression was strongly felt.

After this event, the duo traveled to an impoverished rural area and Robert noted the lack of economic development and the enormous poverty of the area and in particular that the police station was right in the center of this community. Robert and Rigo visited several other barrios and then traveled to Madeira, where Rigo's family lives, to visit with them before traveling on to Africa.

On August 7 they landed in Johannesburg, South Africa, and were picked up by Prince Mashele, a researcher at the Institute for Global Dialogue, the contact that had arranged the South African visit. Their first meeting was at the Institute for Global Dialogue. The following day they traveled to Pretoria and met with the ministers of the labor unions at the Union Building, a palace that is the seat of the South African government.

Between Johannesburg and Pretoria lies the Apartheid Museum. Robert would have liked to spend a great deal more time there, as it was really a visit that should take all day. Hundreds of South Africans, schoolchildren, and tourists visit the Museum everyday. Films that document the anti-apartheid movement that began in 1912 are shown. The African National Congress preceded the Bolshevik uprising in Russia and is the first revolutionary movement of the twentieth century.

On August 13, after touring the area around Johannesburg, a roundtable meeting was held at the Institute for Global Dialogue about the Black Panther Party and the civil rights movement in the United States with twenty-five participants. Many participants asked Robert how South Africa could help in the continuing struggle for civil rights in the United States. They saw their struggles as parallel. There were also lots of questions about Condoleezza Rice, Colin Powell, and Jessie Jackson. He said the general consensus was that the people of America were good people, but the political system was corrupt and rotten with all branches of U.S. government working as one without checks and balances.

Robert spoke on the history of the Black Panther Party and parallels to the ANC struggle in South Africa. He discussed the BPP's internationalist philosophy and the importance of other countries standing up to the U.S. and their imperialist stance, just as it was critical to the ANC's success to have international support.

The following day they visited Luthuli House and met with members of the African National Congress, notably, Secretary General Kgalema Motlante and ANC Director of Foreign Relations Mavivi Mayakayaka-Manzini. After introductions over coffee and tea, the Secretary General made a strong statement of support for the Angola 3. Dr. Motlante, a trade unionist and former political prisoner at Robben Island stated:

> The ANC will use any platform available to us, to do our bit, in assuring that justice will be netted to

> your two compatriots and to help bring into sharp focus the plight of the other political prisoners in the United States. The critical point is this is the starting point. This is the humble starting point, but it has the potential of laying bare, exposing the shortcomings in the entire American system as it were. And, therefore, handled correctly, it could set in motion more or less a chain of events very similar to those inspired by that fateful bus journey by Rosa Parks.

***

The next day Rigo and Robert flew to Durban, where arrangements had been made for Robert to give several presentations on political prisoners in the U.S. and the Angola 3. The first talk was at the University of Natal, "Racism in the United States and the Silencing of the Black Man's Perspective." Although the gathering was primarily academics, Robert felt it was an important talk. Later they went to Westville and stopped at one of the elementary schools, where Robert and Rigo met with many young students. The students were most fascinated by the fact that Robert only spoke one language, as most of them are fluent in at least three languages by the age of ten!

A sightseeing tour the following day took Robert and Rigo to Table Mountain in Cape Town. This mountain is a sacred site and was named because the clouds drape over it like a tablecloth. It sits between the Indian and Atlantic Oceans. They also visited several of the local townships and were moved by the drastically impoverished and squalid conditions they saw. The ANC has begun building houses with the help of Habitat for Humanity in the townships.

Returning to Johannesburg, they attended a special dinner provided by the Institute for Global Dialogue and Mavivi Mayakayaka-Manzini of the ANC attended and spoke. She noted that having Robert there visiting and speaking put a human face on the impact of capitalism. She stressed the ANC's efforts to create a more humane, communalist distribution. South Africa is rich in natural resources — one of the ten richest countries in the world, but much of the wealth is still in the hands of white-owned corporations.

The ANC is a multi-racial party and though currently in the majority, there is a great deal of friction between Zulu's who consider the ANC a disaster and East Indians and whites who still resist the ANC's success.

A tour of Robben Island was a highlight of the trip for Robert. The island lies eight miles off Cape Town and they took a boat trip to this historic site. Two to four boats a day travel to this prison site to pay homage to Nelson Mandela's epic struggle to end apartheid. Robert and Rigo were met by Eddie Daniels, a comrade of Nelson Mandela's who spent fifteen years at Robben Island for sabotage of the apartheid government. Robert said the cells are the same size as those at Angola, but there were no bunks; prisoners were just given a blanket and a bucket. Prisoners at Robben Island broke rocks all day. The governor of the province also lived on Robben Island — a little-known fact! Hillary Clinton had visited recently and was flown by helicopter with a car — unfortunately, the car fell into the ocean en route.

There were only 35-40 prisoners at Robben Island. They were sent there to be forgotten. Prisoners were able to see Table Mountain from the Island and they measured time by the seasons they saw on the mountain.

One of the last speaking events they had was at the University of West Cape, where much of the anti-apartheid struggle commenced through student movements. Robert spoke of the common enemy that they all faced, injustice and oppression. He told students that people always think of the U.S. as heaven, but in heaven there's a corner of hell. In speaking on political prisoners and racism in the U.S. he hoped to change some of their dreams about America. He shared with them his feeling that there was the possibility of many Nelson Mandela's in prisons all over the world. As always, listeners were interested in hearing about the Black Panther Party.

And no . . . Robert and Geronimo never did climb Mt. Kilimanjaro — schedules didn't jibe and there were so many engagements planned that they barely got through all their obligations in the month they spent in South Africa. However, Robert did get to Table Mountain and most importantly, he has a jar full of dirt from Robben Island sitting on the mantle in his home in New Orleans now. Dirt that will forever be a reminder of the potential for positive change that can come from the most hellish of experiences.

Robert King: Thank you very much and thank you all for coming. I just want to give you a brief update on Herman and Albert's case. We saw what happened, the state of Louisiana appealed that conviction and the federal appeals court overturned Albert's conviction. Since that time he has been moved from Angola state prison to another correctional institute about 250 miles away but still in the state of Louisiana, where he is very, very isolated and his status in solitary confinement remains. He, in other words, he still remains in solitary confinement and he . . . [Inaudible as microphone cuts out]

Joe Sim: It's probably my hopelessness with technology, Robert.

This transcript is taken from a talk given by Robert King at the Centre for the Study of Crime, Criminalisation and Social Exclusion, Liverpool, John Moores University, UK, 12 October 2011. The talk was moderated by professor Joe Sim following the showing of the documentary on the Angola 3 *In the Land of the Free*. Thanks to Joe Sim and to Vicky Canning, Vickie Cooper and Samantha Fletcher from the Centre for their efforts in putting the event together. So much of what works brilliantly as spoken word becomes confusing when written down. So while it has been edited for clarity, we hope that none of the force or flavor of hearing King speak live has been lost in the effort.

[Audience laughter; Robert King continues without microphone]

Robert King: Well I think I can go booming, I boom a little bit, I hope you can hear me at the back. Can you hear me at the back?

[Audience: resounding "Yes!"]

Robert King: Yes, well we had trouble with that [points to microphone]. I'll try booming. Yes, so Albert is at Wade correctional institute and he is still in solitary-like conditions. He remains in custody and hopefully some time in January there will be a hearing with the same judge, Judge Brady, who overturned Albert's conviction and recommended that he be released on bail. He has the case again and there is another issue, an error that he can overturn Albert's conviction on.

The current status of Herman's case is that we are now at the fourth stages in the federal court with him and his case, and he is very optimistic. He believes that his case will gravitate along with Albert's although they did not go to trial at the same time. They went up the judicial ladder, but differently. The issues that they had to present are the same, their constitutional rights were violated, from their 4th Amendment rights, you know, which protect you from unlawful intrusion by the state, to 6th Amendment rights being denied — the right to effective assistance of the council which is allegedly allotted to everyone — and also being denied due process which is a 14th Amendment violation.

But having said all of that, we can talk procedure, we can talk about what Buddy Caldwell talked about, but this case is not about any constitutional errors in procedures or the constitution being violated. This case is all about retribution and all about manufacturing evidence against people who were obviously innocent of a crime. There was a rush to judgment.

If you listen to Buddy Caldwell, you would think that he was there on the scene. Matter of fact, Buddy Caldwell had nothing to do with this case initially. His partner John Sinquefield is the person who prosecuted Albert. He was about twenty-five or thirty years senior of Buddy Caldwell. What happened is that John Sinquefield went on to make a career out of prosecutory misconduct, and Albert's case is one of those cases, and Herman's case is one of those cases. He has made a career, and that career has been validated by the fact that he has been able to keep Herman and Albert in prison. He moved up the ladder and became a politician, and he became the Attorney General of the state of Louisiana. His assistant Buddy Caldwell now holds the reins. He has now taken the case and he seems to be obsessed with the case. Somehow he's transformed this obsession far beyond probably what John Sinquefield would have done. But I can imagine you can expect this from a man who sometimes thinks he — and I don't have anything against Elvis. I like Elvis Presley you know, I like some of his songs and I don't have anything against him, great singles — but he is a man who's an Elvis impersonator. This is the type of person we're dealing with. He also feels at times that he has been abducted by quote "illegal aliens." This is on record, and this is the man that you have validating and using his irrationality to keep people in prison.

All of the evidence against them has been undermined; we have the judges on our side in this case. It's not that we don't have the judges; the judges are the ones who are keeping this going. We have magistrates both from the state and the federal level to recommend that both be given a new trial. After Judge Brady's magistrate Christine Noland recommended that Albert be given a new trial, he adopted that conclusion, overturned Albert's case and recommended that he be released unbound. But again Buddy Caldwell stepped in, and you can see his obsession with this case.

But what we want to emphasize, and what we hope to continue to emphasize and focus on, is that we can recount all the procedural errors that we want, this case is based on innocence. We have to continue to focus on the idea that just because something is legal doesn't mean that it is morally and is wholly correct. Legality and morality in the courthouse do not shake hands. There is an adversarial testing ground that a prosecuting attorney should have and a defense attorney should have. They shouldn't be best buddies, you know, going to lunch together and having drinks together and discussing the client and how they're going to sell their client out. Not a case like this. It is a case dealing with morals, the seeds of morality.

When I say morality I don't mean to go into the realm of metaphysics. I don't mean that. I am speaking of the morality that exists, the benevolence, the decency that exists in human beings, the ability to be fair. And I am telling you that the legal system in America, and the world, operates on legal precepts. I don't have anything against legal precepts, but when legal precepts become the deity of society and the God of a society, something is wrong. It was legal to own slaves during chattel slavery in America, but it wasn't until the people saw it as morally reprehensible that something was done about slavery. Prison is an extension of slavery. People say the 13th Amendment abolished slavery but nothing could be further from the truth. The 13th Amendment does not say slavery was a violation and just leave it at that. It went on to say slavery was abolished except for one who has been duly convicted of a crime. How many people in the States have been duly convicted of a crime but are actually totally innocent? So if you are duly convicted of a crime, I mean legally sentenced for a crime, you can become a slave, and if you are legally sentenced to death they can kill you. They did it to Troy Davis. We all know he was legally incarcerated, but morally all of the evidence showed that he was actually innocent.

So I don't have anything against legal precepts if they are implemented with some moral fortitudes in there, some moral aspects, but if you just have a system based on legality, they can kill you. The system can kill you legally, but you will be morally innocent.

I'll open it up to questions, thank you.

Audience member: I just wanted to know, when you were in solitary confinement in CCR, how was it possible throughout your time in solitary confinement to organize, to communicate with your other prisoners about collective issues you had or concerning the Black Panther Party, how do you do it, how did you manage that?

Robert King: We managed to communicate. We were all in cells and they tried to quell and dispel and, you know, keep us from communicating. But we communicated all right. They wanted to make it apparent that they did not want us to communicate to each other and they did it through writing us up, saying that we were talking or being boisterous or being loud, and so forth and so on. There wasn't any written law, but there was an unwritten law against our communicating.

At camp J, which was where I spent two years, there was an unwritten law which they imposed much more than they did at CCR. They did not want you to talk, period, and if you talked they would take you from that spot and put you in another spot. Depending on who you were, you probably were sent away with a couple of broken bones and so forth and so on, and they felt they could get away with it. So they tried to dispel and they tried to keep people from communicating, but I think with the will to communicate we were able to do it.

Audience member: Did you have music? Did you have music at all?

Robert King: Well yes. Death row was in the same area and during that time if you could afford a radio there was music. There was a station that they had in Angola where they played music in certain areas all day every day.

But if you were in solitary confinement, what we call solitary confinement — I think what I really need to do is maybe I need to dispel the concept of what solitary confinement is. I think some people have the concept that solitary confinement is like you see in the old films, the old films way back 300 years ago where they would put people in the dungeon and they would just lock the doors and lock them away. The Quakers used that type of solitary confinement, but this type of solitary confinement only went on for six months. They believed that if they placed a person in that type of environment, kept them away from society for six months, they would go crazy or they would become so remorseful that they would never ever ever commit another crime. The courts eventually eliminated that form of solitary confinement. The difference in Angola, and now America, is that they took it and brought it to a different level. They said, well all right, this is what we are going to do. We are going to take you and put you in a cell for twenty-three hours a day. We are going to minimize what you can have. You're going to be in there for the rest of your life, and if you went to Angola you were in prison for the rest of your life. So if you were in prison way back then, a victim of solitary confinement when it was first invented by the Quakers, you were going to be out in six months if you didn't go crazy. In Angola, Louisiana and in America you could do sixty years in the form of solitary confinement that they have established and never get out.

So I just wanted to point out that solitary confinement in America is not the type of solitary confinement that you see in old movies. The solitary confinement in America is the type that keeps you away twenty-three hours a day, sometimes twenty-four. That limits you, everywhere you go you're shackled and you're handcuffed, and sometimes you get punished for communicating, but guys communicated right on. At one time we were allowed twelve books and one time we were allowed six books. Sometimes we were not allowed contact visits at all. You know, this is what goes on in prison. They have different categories and different rules, and they are different depending on where you are. There are also different statuses of solitary confinement.

Audience member: If you weren't Black Panthers, if you weren't as politicized as you were, do you think you would have been treated as you were? Do you know what I mean? If politics wasn't involved as much?

Robert King: Well, I'm sure it was political. I was not in prison when the security guard was slain. I was 150 miles away. Nevertheless they investigated me for 29 years. I never met the man in my life, but I was investigated for this crime not because I was there, not because I was a co-conspirator, but because I was a member of the Black Panther Party. So was it politics? Yes it was politics.

Audience member: What did you read that most inspired you in prison?

Robert King: Well, I didn't discriminate (laughs). Sometimes you couldn't really get any writing, but I was introduced to the type of writing that I never ever saw in the school that I went to, you know. I met Mao, Che, George Jackson, Richard Wright, all the writers of the twentieth century. Also all these people who had written books way back I didn't know anything about, like Frederick Douglass, Harriet Tubman, Siddhartha. They eventually moved them and put them in the library, but before going to the library I read them. So which is the most inspirational book that I read? I think if I was asked I would say George Jackson's prison letters inspired me, but I can't choose. I see all these books that I've read, I just name all the brothers and I could go on infinity naming the books that I've read. It is hard to say which one was more inspirational, because I think all of them contributed to my evolution. I enjoy all of them.

Audience member: Do you think that keeping them still in prison is more a political view of the American government, so it's not showing the inhumane way which prisons are treated constantly in America, so they are not embarrassed? I'm just saying, is it keeping the prisoners, your friends in America, keeping them in prison more to save the embarrassment of the American government so the inhumanity of it all is not shown?

Robert King: Well, you know the American government has weathered embarrassment and it continues. Of course, keeping people like that in prison, innocent people in prison, should be an embarrassment to the American government, but the American government just doesn't care. I think people in society need to refocus on prison. Not just in America, because our problem goes beyond America because America has influence on a lot of policies around the world. So this is why I believe that people around the world also have to be concerned about what goes on in America, because sometimes where America goes, everyone goes. Almost like the blind leading the blind. But I do believe this, that there are people who can prevent this, people who are dissident people who make their voices and their dissent known. It can't wait until it impacts you directly. Once a pebble is in a pond the ripple can go for positivity or it can go for negativity, so I wouldn't wait to be concerned. Some people think, well, why is he complaining? Some people say America is heaven. People have a right to their prerogative, but I was born and raised in America and I say yes America is heaven to some, but I let people know that in heaven they got some people kept in hell.

[Audience applause]

Audience member: Do you think African Americans will ever have justice in America or will they continue to be oppressed?

Robert King: Ah, okay, justice. I think that the foundation . . . justice is evolving, you know what I'm saying? I can look at the Communist Party Manifesto or I can look at the U.S. Constitution and the words are so beautiful. It is the implementation of the words, that and the people who get in the way. It's okay to compartmentalize and separate and look at this like this but I have evolved to a point of connecting the dots and I see everything as connected. I think that injustice for African Americans is equally an injustice for so many other people, because they have been deceived and taught to accept and embrace a way that is so unholy until it does injustice to them. So, you know, looking at it like that, I have a much broader perspective. So when you say do I believe that African Americans will ever achieve justice, I think justice is an ongoing thing. I think justice is evolving, I don't think it's stagnant. I think there are "people" and "Black people" in America because America has a history of discriminating against people based on skin color, because a construct was constructed based on skin color. I think that in the end, the ability to achieve justice eludes them much more than it does other people who are also victims of injustice. I believe we are all victims of politics.

When I say politics I think this especially is true for America. The politics of America tell you America is a democracy. Democracy for who? It's democracy for people who are rich, corporate democracy. There is no true democracy. Even the middle class, who may have tasted a little democracy, has been eroded. Democracy gives people power, it comes from the Greek word for power, but people don't have power. With people not having power, they don't have justice either. They have a legal right to vote for politicians. Will they achieve justice? I think knowledge you know. Racism, discrimination are learnt reflexes, I'm a believer in cause and effect and anything that is learned can be unlearned.

Audience member: Mine is a short one. The media who have such strong influences in society these days. I was just wondering whether you can give us a list, if any, of any of the media outlets, particularly the U.S. media, which have given support to the Angola campaign, media outlets like Sky, CNN, Fox News [audience laughter] and the rest of them, because they are the ones who they are quick to condemn China, human rights abuses, so it would be interesting to know to what extent if at all U.S. media outlets have lent any sort of support to the Angola campaign.

Robert King: Well, NPR has given an extensive review on Angola 3 and CNN also covered it. All of the smaller media around the country have covered it, but in spite of that we are going to continue to try and get more media coverage. You can also go on our website and you can see that we have networks. It's not just in this local stuff, we have national coverage as well and of course we have BBC and other areas like that. But I think the biggest media are propagated by the grassroots. You know, I'm a firm believer in grassroots people. I mean media can suppress things, whichever media you get behind you. But the ideal I think, the biggest media, is the people.

[Audience applause]

Audience member: I'd just like to ask you, you were in prison for a long time, what sort of progress did you see when you came out, how society had changed. Could you actually see progress there?

Robert King: Well once I got out I saw that some of society has changed, but one thing was a great leap in technology that could knock anybody for a loop. So it has changed in that sense. But on the other hand, you know, after a certain time we began to get support while in prison and we began to have people send us information, and asking what was going on with current events we tried our best to keep up with them. So society had undergone a change and transformation, to some people for the better, but to some for the worse. I think that a lot of people were knocked out of the middle class, but a lot of people found consolation in the fact that they were able to maybe acquire what they call a decent living. So, yes, there was a change, there was a transformation, but it was a negative transformation.

Audience member: I'm just wondering how you maintained hope since the execution of Troy Davis, and also what you think about President Obama's inability to grant clemency to him whether he had that power or not?

Robert King: Thank you for the question. What do I think about hope after seeing Troy Davis murdered by the State? I think that where there is no hope, or where hope is doubting, I think that hope should be increased. Of course we have hope. Having hope does not mean that we have any hope in the judicial system or any one individual, but I do think that hope is in the might and power of the people. Herman and Albert will tell you that they have had the hope and the focus of the people, and that this is their buoyancy. This keeps them afloat, so of course they have hope.

I could elaborate further on that, but I know you are waiting on the question on Obama and his quote "inability" to intercede. We have a system. I don't want to rationalize, I like to shoot straight from the hip, you know. We have three systems. We have the executive branch, and Obama who's the president of the United States, who just happens to be a Black in the White House. He's a politician, his first and foremost duty is to the American people — the entire American People — so he focuses on them. Of course he is given the power at Thanksgiving time to pardon a turkey or a federal prisoner, but that same power does not give him the power to pardon a prisoner who has been convicted by the state and who has gone through the courts. It just does not give him that power to do it.

A lot of people believe, by the way, that the Tea Party are a force to be reckoned with. But the Tea Party did not elect Obama to the White House, the Republicans who are denouncing him and who are throwing all types of impediments in his way also did not elect him, the people who elected him are still behind him. I think what he needs to know is that he has a force behind him that is much stronger than all the other opposition you see on Fox News. I'm sorry if there is anybody here from Fox News [audience laughter]. Don't take it personally, you're not under attack, but there is an agenda that Fox has that is unrelated to what the people in the United States have and what democracy is all about. So getting back to the point that there are three separate entities, three separate layers of law with the executive branch at the highest level. You know you also got the legislative branch that consists of congresspeople and representatives, and then you have republicans and democrats, who you got fighting in elections to see who can be a majority. And then there's the law end. We have the judicial branch that deals with criminality, and they are sovereign. And I use that so to speak as they have been given the sovereignty to prosecute, to kill, to enforce slavery through incarceration — by whatever name you're familiar with or want to use. They have this authority and they have this power. And so whilst President Obama has the power to pardon a turkey at Thanksgiving, he don't have that same authority, power of sovereignty to pardon a human being who has been falsely convicted for a crime.

But check this, I am a firm believer of cause and effect. Throw pebbles in a pond, you get ripples. I believe there's a ripple effect in the nation. When I was in Spain a couple of days ago I looked, and while it's not on a lot of the televisions around here, there is a movement against corporate America and corporate capitalism. Now I don't have anything against people capitalism, but corporate capitalism I have a problem with, and that is what has been running America for ages and people are dying as a result of it. But there is a movement, take my word for it. There is a movement in the states against corporate greed and corporate capitalism. I don't care what you hear the Tea Party say or the Republicans say or deny, you will see there is a movement. There is also a movement for the abolishment of the death penalty. Before Troy Davis was executed it was not stagnant, but they were not out front and they did not progress it the way they are doing now. So there is something going on, and I think the reverberations will be felt across the oceans.

[Audience applause]

SHAKA OR CHECKS AND BALANCES

AS THE BOOK WAS FIRST MADE READY TO go to press it was suggested that the original title "A Cry from the Bottom of the Heap" be shortened to "From the Bottom of the Heap." I agreed. In retrospect the original title was rooted in intention: it was deliberate, not to capture the cry of defeat or agony but to capture the cry that follows righteous wrath or dissent. In short it is a cry for action!

The state of Texas had set the date for the murder of Shaka Sankofa, a.k.a. Gary Graham, for the month of June 2000. As the time approached we waited. tense, hopeful that the system would do the right thing. By "we," I mean all of Shaka Sankofa's supporters. As the moments ticked away, not only did we lose hope, we lost Shaka as well. The day was June 22, 2000, when the State of Texas killed him. People both here in this nation and globally had paused, waiting for the inevitable killing of the innocent. Intensely angered at what had transpired, or what justice loving people had seen transpire, I entitled the article "Checks and Balances."

In retrospect it should not have reached the point described above. For Shaka was obviously innocent, just as obviously, he was "fair game." When we consider the countervailing exculpatory evidence omitted or unavailable during his trial, not only does this evidence show that Shaka was juridically innocent, but it shows he was probably actually innocent as well. His prosecutors knew this; and the rest of the listening and caring world later learned it too. What became quite evident in Shaka's situation is that from the time of his initial arrest in 1981, through his ensuing nineteen years on death row, the system of checks and balances was well on its way to becoming incapable (or unwilling) of checking and balancing itself, especially in the criminal justice arena.

The legislative branch began failing when, in exercising its prerogative, it enacted laws limiting the defendant's access to the courts, even for those espousing claims of actual innocence. The executive branch added to this failure when, not caring about the negative ramifications these new laws would have on the unfortunate — or innocent — defendant, they signed these bills into law. The judicial branch aided and abetted this failure when, in its condescending rhetoric, it implicitly asserted that "innocence is irrelevant," or that innocence is not a constitutional claim. Claiming and showing actual innocence is not enough and does not give a court of law any legal reason to void a conviction if no constitutional violation occurred during the trial. If this sounds like double-speak, that is exactly what it is. It has become an obvious trademark of the judiciary.

By the time Shaka was killed, the system had come full circle in negating itself by showing its incapability of righting an obvious wrong. The executive branch headed by the then-president Clinton in Washington alas failed. The lesser branch of state government headed by cold, callous, calculating (falsely labeled "compassionate conservative") George W. Bush, was content to "chill out" and let the killing take place. In fact George W. Bush, while governor of Texas executed more people than any of his predecessors. Of course, Bush's successor, Governor Perry of Texas, has already surpassed Bush's record for the number of executions.[1]

The legislative branch, still on a collision course with morality, exercised its amoral prerogative. The judicial branch is reputed

1. The State of Texas killed 152 people under George W. Bush when he was governor of Texas, but by the end of 2011, Texas had executed another 236 people under Rick Perry. The *Texas Tribune* has put together a good factual visualization that you can see here: http://www.texastribune.org/texas-people/rick-perry/under-perry-executions-raise-questions/.

to be the last bastion or bulwark of the three branches which allegedly assures life, liberty and due process, and whose function is to correct, check, and balance when the other two fail. Alas, it succumbed to its own rhetoric. It should be noted here that when this branch of the government fails, after all others have failed, the victims have no one to turn to but themselves.

At the time this predicted an ill omen. The fact that states are able to kill with such impunity should not sit well with anyone, but especially not with twenty-first-century activists who seriously disapprove of state killings and repression. Since Shaka's execution, the United States has continued to execute many people to this day. Most notable is the State of Georgia murdering Troy Davis.[2] It was Troy's wish that we continue to seek abolition of the death penalty.

On the night Troy was scheduled to be killed, I was in Pittsburgh, PA, speaking to an audience who also waited for news of Troy's fate. The time ticked away. I felt that vibration of my phone, a call from a friend in California who I had asked to monitor that night's event. His voice said excitedly, "We got a stay." We soon learned that the stay was temporary. The State of Georgia executed its 52nd prisoner, Troy Davis.[3] It was Troy's last wish that we continue the struggle against State executions.

From the time Shaka was murdered in 2000, through to the time Troy Davis was killed by the State of Georgia in 2012, the U.S. has executed 484 prisoners.[4] This must give us pause for national and rational reflection regarding the need to abolish the death penalty. MSNBC commentator Laurence O'Donnell has said in part if we want to eliminate the death penalty, we can't just focus on those cases where people are innocent, we have to seek to abolish the death penalty period. I agree. We have to seek abolition of the death penalty in all cases, whether the person is

2. See http://www.amnestyusa.org/our-work/usa-troy-davis for more information on Troy Davis's innocence and last wishes.
3. http://en.wikipedia.org/wiki/List_of_people_executed_in_Georgia_(U.S._state).
4. http://www.deathpenaltyinfo.org/documents/FactSheet.pdf.

innocent or guilty. As long as we live in a system of legal precepts where legality, not innocence or justice, is god, such as we saw in the case of Troy, people will be brought to trial, found legally guilty, and legally murdered.

As long as the death sentence is on the roster, there will be persons who are found guilty legally and killed by the state legally. It is the legal precept that killed them. Legality gives the state the right to make "them pay for their crime," either through execution or by keeping them imprisoned in solitary confinement for the remainder of their natural lives. It is no accident that those most impacted by this kind of "legality" are the poor and people of color, given the severe racial disparities that have been documented in the legal process from jury selection to sentencing to treatment while in prison.[5]

A final word I would like to say regarding the death penalty. There are three valid personal reasons that I feel the death penalty should be abolished. They are: Albert Woodfox, Herman Wallace, and myself. In 1972, in *Furman v. Georgia*, the United States Supreme Court placed a moratorium on carrying out death sentences. Had that decision not been rendered, neither Albert, Herman, nor myself would be on the planet today. The State of Louisiana would have executed us on the subsequent murder convictions received while in prison. The moratorium put a pause on executions for the crime of murder for which we were all charged. All capital crimes which ordinarily would require a sentence of death was temporarily reduced to the more "responsive verdict," which was a life sentence. Had not the high court allowed the window of a life sentence, Albert, Herman, and I would have been executed. The State of Louisiana's "rush to judgment" in prosecuting us would have cost us our lives.

---

5. http://takeaction.amnestyusa.org/atf/cf/%7B4abebe75-41bd-4160-91dd-a9e121f0eb0b%7D/DEATHPENALTYFACTS-OCTOBER2011.PDF.

WHAT'S IN A NAME . . . (VULGARIZING . . . VULGARITY)

THE FOLLOWING PIECE IS AN ARTICLE written while still in prison. Unfortunately my last copy was lost in the aftermath of Hurricane Katrina, so I have had to reconstruct it. I initially entitled it "Vulgarizing Vulgarity," i.e., the further vulgarizing of the word "negro" by extending its uses to "nigger" etc. Some will argue and say that the word "negro" is not vulgar when it comes to describing people of African descent. I disagree.

It was my wish to include this writing, as well as the article entitled "Checks and Balances" (which has been extended to cover the State of Georgia's killing of Troy Davis as well as the State of Texas's killing of Shaka Sankofa, a.k.a. Garry Graham, 11 years earlier) in the first edition of the book, but my wish was also to have more time for revision. It now appears in this second edition and I have entitled it "What's in a Name" with the subtitle "Vulgarizing . . . Vulgarity."

Names have meanings. The word "negro" derives from the Spanish dialect, however, like most languages the Castilian dialect also takes its meaning from roots found in the Greek language. Some words in different languages share the same meaning. For example "negro" and "necro" are two such words. In the Greek language the word "negro" is pronounced "necro," which means something that is dead or decaying. Similarly, the word in the Spanish language has the same meaning. Additionally, no other word in the English language has as many negative connotations as the word "negro." Roget's Thesaurus has more than two dozen synonyms for "black" or "negro"; all are negative. Conversely, no other word in the English language has generated so much negative stigma as the word "negro" and its variants.

History tells us that when European traders sailed to Africa in the fifteenth century and were greeted by its African inhabitants, their initial description of the darker folks they encountered was undoubtedly influenced by their dialect. They called them "negros." So we can presume here that the word was and is colonial. Nevertheless, despite having no prior land base in Africa, the word "negro" became synonymous with people of African descent. Some writers and scholars have written and argued that the word has origins or that it originated in Africa, citing the Niger River and the Nigerian nation in an attempt to provide the heredity of the word. Also, the name "negus," ancient Ethiopian "King Of Kings," is often used or cited as proof of heredity. Books galore have been written on "negritude" (or "The Pulchritude of Negritude") in further attempts to prove heredity. Proof of heredity does not exist. So again, despite having no prior land base in Africa, despite their being no place called "negroland," the word "negro" became synonymous with people of African descent.

Still later, anthropologists got involved: classifying the human species into racial categories: "Whites/Caucasians," "Asians/Mongoloids," and "Africans/Negroids." With this pseudoscientific spin added, uses of the word "negro" became pandemic and worldwide. We can assume that people of the African continent have denounced their synonymy with the word. In fact Malcolm X, in bringing the plight of the so-called Negro to the OAU (Organization of African Unity) by using the term negro, was reminded by leaders of the OAU that they did not cater to the term "negro." It was then that Malcolm X began using the term African or Afro-American. However, for their descendants brought to North America and other parts of the world as slaves, the word "negro" and its variants evolved with the infrastructure: prefixing churches, schools, colleges, universities, sorority clubs, on into infinity. While the word "negro" permeates the languages of the world, it should be noted that in North America, particularly in the Southern states where chattel slavery was rampant, racists took the word and its variants to another level.

In time, acceptability of the word permeated the entire world. This also led to acceptability of all its variants. People of African descent began to use the variants more frequently than anyone else, wearing them as if they were a second skin. But while white racists in the South took the word and its variants to one level, pop culture, and the hip hoppers took this word (and a few other words) to an even greater level. Music to this day blares loudly, repeating the word in psycho-cadence, as if having the word hammered into the subconscious will somehow numb its true meaning.

Can you imagine how ludicrous (and dangerous, I may add) it would be for anyone who attempted to glamorize these terms: (ofay, hymie, dago, spic, wop, chink etc.) in songs or in any other form?[1] All of these terms are racial slurs and none would be tolerated today, or otherwise perpetuated in the manner in which we have perpetuated "negro" and its variants. This is not an indictment of pop or hip-hop culture; long before their casual uses of the word, it was already rampant amongst people of Africa descent. Assessing this history, one can perhaps understand the younger generations' attempt to try and neutralize the word through overexposure, as if this would somehow numb our senses to its true meaning. Attempting to put a pig in a suit and necktie to make it acceptable does not make it acceptable; it is still a pig. The point is that no matter how much "dressing" we attempt to put on the word "negro" or its variants, they are still vulgar, demeaning, and unpalatable. There are some lemons that cannot be converted into lemonade.[2]

1. The author's uses of terms which are considered offensive are used only for literary references and in no way are intended to offend any individual or group who may find the use of any one of these words offensive.
2. Again, I want to emphasize that this is not an indictment against pop culture/hip-hop culture. For it is the hip-hop/pop culture that has bridged the gap between the two oceans, bringing folks of all beats together. I've been

I am here reminded of a story that surfaced in the mid 1980s somewhere in the Southern States: Louisiana or Mississippi. There was a young African-American student. I don't remember his name. However, I do know that his name was not "nigger." There was another young man of European descent who insisted on calling the young man "nigger." After being repeatedly called by this name, a fight ensued, and the young man of European descent was unfortunately killed. Needless to say the young man went to trial, his only defense being that his name wasn't "nigger." While sentencing him to natural life in prison, the white judge reminded the young man that Black folks used that word all the time. Sadly, the judge was right.

I have often wondered over the years where the young man went, and I have wondered whether he survived as I knew that in prison he would be spending the rest of his natural life hearing that word directed at him on a daily basis by people who looked just like him. He learned at an early age that the word and its variants were not representative of him or people of African descent. However in embracing this truth he paid dearly for it, learning that to whom much is given, much is required, and that when you increase knowledge you increase sorrow. He became a modern-day Atlas as he bore the world on his shoulders; I hope he did not succumb to the weight.

Around the same time the judge was giving a life sentence to the student, another white judge (I believe it was in the state of Florida) was granting a civil suit to a white woman who had sued a Black man. The judge ruled that she had proven that her encounter with the Black man had triggered her phobia: I think the judge called it "negro-phobia."

---

to some of the deepest recesses of this planet and covered five continents. My "rights of passage" to certain areas was, did I know Tupac, or had I been a "Black Panther"? Finally, it is relevant to say here that the establishment itself has recognized the apparent influence ignored by others — the influence hip-hop culture was having on America and the rest of the world. In fact, in the early 1990s there was a call in government to investigate the hip-hop movement in the same way that the Black Panthers and other groups were targeted and subjected to systemic intrusions.

THE FABLE OF THE MONKEY AND THE LION

Once upon a time the lion was believed to be the king of the jungle. This was believed by all of the animals in the jungle except one. The lone standout was the monkey, also known as Mimic, so named because he could imitate almost any other creature accept the lion. The lion, the monkey reasoned, was cunning and brutally strong, but for all his strength the monkey knew that this strength was utilized only for food. Other than that, monkey reasoned, this "Mr. Mighty King of the Jungle" was too trusting and too honest. The lion's main thought was instant food. Once having eaten, the lion was satisfied. While the monkey's thought was also about food, the monkey's main concern was about the lion being the King of the Jungle. The monkey did not believe it and set out to disprove it. High and bye the monkey developed a plan . . .

Deceit would be the monkey's main weapon. Initially monkey went into this matter as a jokester going through the jungle telling everyone (except the lion of course), that he was the true King of the Jungle. Monkey would meet others and say, "Hey, have you heard the news?" and, without waiting for an answer, go on to explain that "Mr. Lion is always declaring that he is a monkey's uncle. The truth of the matter is that the so called King of Jungle is in fact a monkey's uncle."

The monkey had scouted the lion and knew that one of his habits was that when he was surprised or flabbergasted he retorted loudly "Well, I'll be a monkeys uncle." Now the monkey, along with hundreds of other animals in the jungle, had heard this from the lion all of the time. This too is another reason why the monkey did not like the lion, declaring itself a "Monkey's Uncle" was insulting and belittling to the monkey. The monkey went on to tell the other animals that the lion was really a monkey and the monkey was in fact a lion. Those to whom the monkey uttered these words would initially laugh, because all the animals in the jungle knew who the real king of the jungle was. But this went on for years and years and so what had started out as a joke, actually ended up being seen as a fact. All lions now considered themselves to be monkeys, and the monkeys now considered themselves to be lions. Soon throughout the entire jungle the switching of names became official: all monkeys became lions and all lions became monkeys. Until this day in the jungle, the true lions, still mighty, still strong, still have the mightiest roar. But having relinquished its true name, it repeats the moniker given him by monkey, insisting beyond all rationality that "monkey" is its true name, and the monkey likewise calls itself a lion.

The above is just a fable. We all know what a fable is. A monkey cannot adorn itself in a lion's apparel and suddenly become a lion. Neither can a lion become a monkey. Instead, the end result is that both suffer from a severe identity crisis. "In the jungle, the mighty jungle, the lion sleeps tonight . . . Hush my darlin', don't fear my darlin', the lion sleeps tonight . . . "[3]

3. Solomon Linda and the Evening Birds, 1939.

APPENDICES

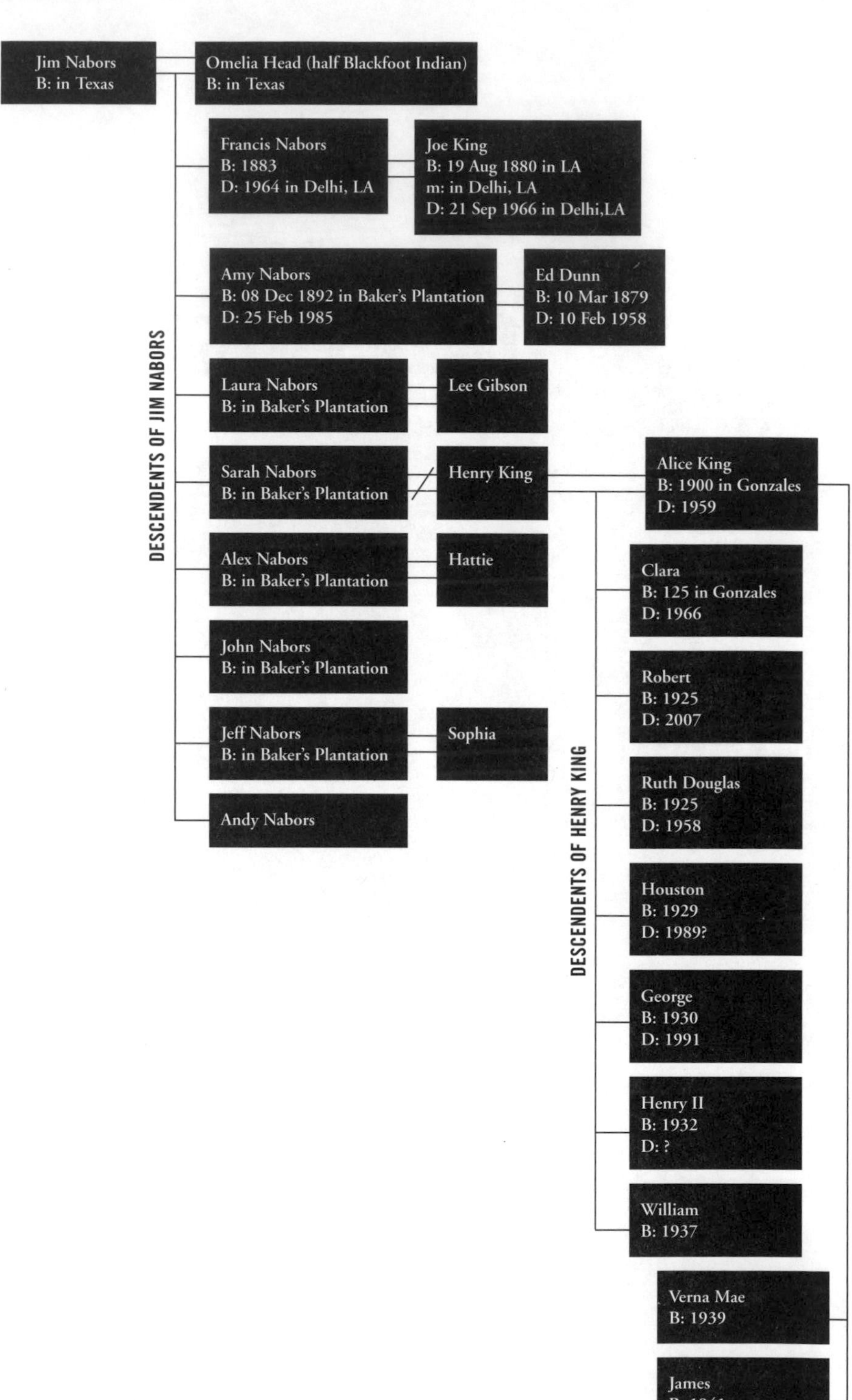
Jim Nabors
B: in Texas
Omelia Head (half Blackfoot Indian)
B: in Texas
DESCENDENTS OF JIM NABORS
Francis Nabors
B: 1883
D: 1964 in Delhi, LA
Joe King
B: 19 Aug 1880 in LA
m: in Delhi, LA
D: 21 Sep 1966 in Delhi,LA
Amy Nabors
B: 08 Dec 1892 in Baker's Plantation
D: 25 Feb 1985
Ed Dunn
B: 10 Mar 1879
D: 10 Feb 1958
Laura Nabors
B: in Baker's Plantation
Lee Gibson
Sarah Nabors
B: in Baker's Plantation
Henry King
Alice King
B: 1900 in Gonzales
D: 1959
Alex Nabors
B: in Baker's Plantation
Hattie
John Nabors
B: in Baker's Plantation
Jeff Nabors
B: in Baker's Plantation
Sophia
Andy Nabors
DESCENDENTS OF HENRY KING
Clara
B: 125 in Gonzales
D: 1966
Robert
B: 1925
D: 2007
Ruth Douglas
B: 1925
D: 1958
Houston
B: 1929
D: 1989?
George
B: 1930
D: 1991
Henry II
B: 1932
D: ?
William
B: 1937
Verna Mae
B: 1939
James
B: 1941

KING FAMILY TREE

HENRY KING, MY MATERNAL GRANDFATHER, was the son of Wyatt King, known as the "African" because he is believed to be the Kings' direct link to Africa. Wyatt settled down in Louisiana and married Lucy Williams. They had eight children: Racheal, Lily, Ora, C.L., "Crocke," Henry, Joe, and Bloom, in that order. My grandfather was number six. It is not exactly known where or when my grandfather was born. However, gauging from the information gathered, Henry was born around 1885. He married Sarah Nabors (in Baker's Plantation). No search has been conducted in regards to children, if any, of this marriage between Henry and Sarah. Around 1923, he started having a relationship with Alice, my grandmother, who at the time, having previously married (as a child bride) to a Phillip Earle, was still in her teens. Alice had had no children from her previous marriage. From the marital bond between Henry and Alice came seven children: my mother Clara (being the first), Robert and Ruth (fraternal twins), Houston, George, Henry King Jr., and William. Alice would later have two more children: Verna Mae and James King.

ANITA RODDICK: A FRIEND OF DISTINCTION

I'VE HAD MANY DAYS TO REFLECT AND TO ruminate on the untimely departure of a friend of distinction, Anita Roddick. She was a friend to the planet, a friend to the environment, a friend to the downtrodden. She was both a friend of mine, and a friend to the Angola 3. I am here today as the only freed member of the Angola 3 to pay tribute, and to participate in the memorial of my friend, our friend, a true friend of distinction who brought hope to so many. She even brought hope to Angola State Prison in the United States of America. When Anita heard of our collective plight in Angola and prisons throughout America, she became first enraged, and then engaged herself in becoming a friend through the struggle.

My first recollection of Anita was at a dinner in 2003, in midtown New Orleans. She was a ball of energy, forever talking, laughing, and smiling. She was always just Anita. There were subsequent dinners and meetings as Anita's quest to "free the Angola 3" heightened, and she increased her visits to Angola Prison, to meet and visit with Albert and Herman regularly. She also elevated her efforts to bring Herman and Albert to the rest of the world. She succeeded! This ever greater effort was paused by her sudden transition. But in pausing, there have been some reflections. Those reflections have revealed that, with her husband Gordon and family at the helm, Anita's fire will continue to burn brightly, illuminating the walls, prison bars, and halls of injustice that hold her friends captive.

Anita took it personally. She looked at this monster in America. She saw the criminal in-justice system that is gobbling up so many of America's minority youth, criminalizing whole generations, splitting families apart, and perpetuating a permanent underclass. She recognized it for what it was: slavery. Without Anita's passion, it's quite possible the Angola 3 would have remained obscured from the broader public view.

So let me say, we are here today for you, Anita. You left us a great legacy, but the memory of you is greater! No mourning, you would not want that . . . though I must confess quite a few of us cried anyway. I am sure you will forgive us. Please know that we are mindful of the legacy of struggle you left us. Because we love you and want to honor your memory, we know that it is imperative for us to continue walking your talk. For you yourself not only talked the talk, you walked your talk. We're sending one of our family home to the ancestors. From Herman, Albert and all the Angola 3 supporters, we say ashe' to a revolutionary comrade who has made her transition.

A POEM FOR ALICE (AFRICA)

. . . A WOMAN. THE TRUE WOMAN. THE Amazon. The Queen and Mother of the planet Earth. A Women whose greatness exceeds that of time itself. She gave birth to Kings of Egypt, and of Nubia: gave birth to Queens of Egypt and Ethiopia; to countless number of Princes and Princesses. She has been awarded the Noble Prize by Wisdom itself for her birth of the first civilization (and generation). She was Black; She is beautiful . . .

. . . Her name is Africa. Because of Her selfless nature, She welcomed strangers with outstretched arms. And because of Her multitude of kindnesses, Her magnanimous spirit, and Her longsuffering nature, those strangers looked upon Her as being simple . . .

. . . From far away places, they looked upon Her beauty which was a sight to behold! Lo! In time they came. Along with them came lust, greed, jealousy, and all manner of foul intent. They seized the symbol of beauty! Begun ravishing Her! Carried her seed by force into strange lands . . .

. . . They placed a ransom on Her and Her seed. And though this ransom has been paid many times over to the abductors, by Her and Her seed, the cries for freedom have gone unheeded, have become a byword, an object of contempt!

. . . Aiee! She is a righteous, longsuffering Woman; She is slow to anger, but rage undammed! Her powers, which are indeed mighty—are likened unto the rolling and coming together of many waters. With a determination to match Her many powers, she will free herself from her abductors. Her seed will free itself also. The cries of victory and freedom for all will then be heard throughout the world!

MALIK RAHIM AND THE FOUNDING OF COMMON GROUND

MALIK RAHIM WAS AMONG THE FIRST Panthers arrested by the New Orleans police. He was acquitted, but he remains an advocate for justice and prisoners' rights, and spearheaded the efforts to garner support for Herman Wallace, Albert Woodfox, and myself. Enough could never be written about his undying work to claim justice for the downtrodden.

Both Malik and I were living in New Orleans when Katrina hit in 2005. While Malik was on higher ground in Algiers, my own place in mid-city was almost completely flooded. And you could say that Common Ground arose out of scott crow's efforts to find me.

Scott set out from Austin and Dallas to find me at my home. His initial effort failed. But, undaunted, he set out once again three days later. Scott stayed with Malik in Algiers, where they formulated the idea for an organization to deal with the crisis at hand.

Armed rangers in the area came to my house, and this time I decided to leave as they allowed me to bring my dog Kenya. I then met up with Malik, scott, and Sharon Johnson who were already working to found Common Ground. Malik used his home as a shelter and distribution center, and the organization to this day has been a key factor in the creation of shelters and distribution centers, and in providing the necessities of life in the absence of government support such as health clinics, legal assistance, and bio remediation efforts. Much has been written about Katrina and Common Ground, and scott crow's description of its founding, successes, and failures, *Black Flags and Windmills: Hope, Anarchy, and the Common Ground Collective*, has now been published.

I believe that Common Ground — and other relief organizations arising out of a necessity created by federal, state, and local government neglect — could very well become catalysts of significant grassroots organization. They offer political alternatives and solutions to problems long faced by the poor, but a word of caution, however. Common Ground should not make the mistakes of past "catalysts" by allowing itself to become a fixed and therefore static organization without the potential to grow and keep growing with the needs of the people. Common Ground started out as a radical organization; radicalism in the aftermath of Katrina is required, and Common Ground needs to remain so.

The emergence of Common Ground also gives us a deeper insight into the perception of young (and not so young) white Americans. More than 90 percent of the volunteers in New Orleans since Katrina have been young, white radicals whose continued presence suggests their radical stance. It also suggests that these young radicals will no longer tolerate the oppression of those less privileged in society. Most importantly, it strongly suggests that the time is right for young (and not so young) African-Americans to examine their strategy of excluding whites from the struggle for fear of whites taking over. Common Ground is an organization started by Malik and Sharon Johnson, both African-Americans, and scott crow, who is white. Together, they are telling our government "not anymore, not in our name, not on our watch." In the aftermath of Katrina, I have met whites willing to sacrifice their unearned privilege, their health, and, most importantly, their lives. More about Common Ground and its continued effort to aid victims in New Orleans and other Katrina affected areas can be found at www.commongroundrelief.org.

THE CASE OF THE ANGOLA 3

THIRTY-SIX YEARS AGO, THREE YOUNG Black men deep in rural Louisiana named Robert King, Herman Wallace and Albert Woodfox formed a prison chapter of The Black Panther Party. They were silenced for trying to expose continued segregation, systematic corruption, and horrific abuse in the biggest prison in the US: the 18,000-acre former slave plantation called Angola.

Peaceful, non-violent protest in the form of hunger and work strikes organized by inmates, caught the attention of prison, state and federal officials.

In the early 1970s prison officials, targeted them for their activism and determined to put an end to their activities. They framed Herman Wallace, Albert Woodfox, and Robert King with murders they did not commit and threw them into 6x9 foot cells in solitary confinement, for over thirty years. Robert was exonerated and freed in 2001, but Herman and Albert who spent nearly thirty-six years in solitary, having just been moved to "temporary quarters" after intense public pressure, are still serving life sentences remain behind bars.

Their cases have drawn the support of the A.C.L.U. (American Civil Liberties Union) and Amnesty International, and Senator John Conyers head of the House Judiciary Committee for the violations to their basic human rights.

There have been some breakthroughs in the campaign since Robert King proved his innocence and walked free in 2001.

September 19, 2006

Judicial Commissioner Rachel Morgan recommended overturning Herman's conviction, finding the trial fundamentally unfair because Wallace was prevented from demonstrating Hezekiah Brown's motive for testifying to the jury. Among other perks, Brown was paid a carton of cigarettes a week, used as prison currency, and eventually rewarded with a pardon and release from prison.

March 26, 2008

Following a visit from U.S. House Judiciary Committee Chairman John Conyers Jr., Herman Wallace and Albert Woodfox were transferred from solitary after 36 years to a specially created and hastily built dorm that holds 20 men. Sen. Conyers and Cedric Richmond Chairman, who heads the House Judiciary Committee in Louisiana, have called for an investigation into the cases as well as into the "prosecutorial misconduct and corruption" of prison officials.

March 24, 2008

Only 4 days after U.S. House Judiciary Chair Congressman John Conyers, State Judiciary Committee Chair Rep. Cedric Richmond, and renowned Innocence Project founder Barry Scheck made a historic visit to Angola, prison officials moved Herman and Albert from solitary to a maximum security dormitory after 35 years, 11 months, and 7 days alone in 6x9-foot cells.

May 15, 2008

In a 2-1 decision, the First Circuit Court of Appeals denied Herman's appeal despite Commissioner Morgan's September 2006 recommendation. The majority failed to give any reason for their decision, while Judge Welch the dissenting voice said, "There was a reasonable likelihood that the verdict would have been different had the jury been aware of the promise and favors to the state's witness," and that the State's failure to disclose this information violated Herman's constitutional rights.

June 10, 2008

Federal Magistrate Christine Noland of the U.S. District Court for the Middle District of Louisiana recommended the reversal of Albert Woodfox's conviction for the murder of Brent Miller due to numerous court and prosecutorial misconduct incidents in his 1998 retrial.

September 25, 2008

U.S. District Judge James Brady overturned Albert Woodfox's conviction for the 1972 murder of Brent Miller. This was the second time his conviction was overturned (the first in 1996) by judges citing racial discrimination, prosecutorial misconduct, inadequate defense, and suppression of exculpatory evidence.

November 13, 2008

Only eight months after being released from solitary, Herman and Albert were again separated and thrown back into solitary dungeons "pending investigation" of a minor rule violation. They have remained in solitary since.

March 18, 2009

Herman was transferred to Elayn Hunt Correctional Center Prison two hours south of Angola, where he remains under the control of Angola Warden Burl Cain, who also serves as regional warden.

October 9, 2009

The Louisiana Supreme Court refused to review the May 2008 appeals court decision that rejected the report and recommendation of the magistrate judge who found Herman's trial to be unconstitutional and recommended vacating his conviction. Herman's attorneys appealed to the federal courts, where it is still under consideration.

June 21, 2010

The United States Court of Appeals for the Fifth Circuit reversed Judge Brady's decision and reinstated Albert's conviction largely based on the AEDPA (Anti-Terrorism and Effective Death Penalty Act), a Clinton-era law that guts habeas protections by limiting federal power.

November 1, 2010

Albert was moved from Angola to David Wade Correctional Center, four hours north of Angola.

April 17, 2012

This day marked 40 years in solitary confinement for Herman Wallace and Albert Woodfox. An official commemoration took place at the State Capitol in Baton Rouge, Louisiana. Amnesty International, Robert King and Angola 3 supporters handed in a global petition to Governor Jindal demanding Herman and Albert's immediate release from solitary confinement.

June 1, 2012

This day brought a close to a 3-day federal hearing again in front of Federal District Judge James Brady to determine whether Albert's conviction should be overturned for a third time based on racial discrimination in the Grand Jury Foreperson selection process during his 1998 retrial. A decision is expected by the end of 2012.

Civil Case

In addition, the Angola 3 civil rights suit, which alleges that their 36+ years as well as Robert King's 29 years in solitary confinement is a violation of the "right to due process" and amounts to "cruel and unusual punishment" as set forth in the U.S. Constitution. The suit, which the United States Supreme Court ruled 'has merit to proceed' in 2004, is moving forward in federal court and could go to trial in the fall of this year.

In addition to King's release, these developments are the biggest to happen in the years of being held behind bars.

The future is unwritten . . .

For more information on the cases of the Angola 3, updates on Herman and Albert, and to write them please visit:
www.Angola3.org
www.3BlackPanthers.org
www.A3grassroots.org

Since his release from Angola, Robert King has been working on his own candy business called King's Freelines. He explained how he came to start it in one of the all-time requested episodes of hosts Davia Nelson and Nikki Silva's Kitchen Sisters' *Hidden Kitchens* on National Public Radio. It aired shortly after Hurricane Katrina in 2005 and was featured on the front page of the *Austin American-Statesman* in 2006. He explained:

In 1962, at Angola Prison in Louisiana I learned to concoct a special praline-like candy from a fellow prisoner named "Cap Pistol." I continued to make this recipe of sugar, butter, milk and pecans, even during the twenty-nine years I spent in restricted confinement. In my cell, I made my candy using a stove of stacked tin cans, and tissue for fuel. The ingredients came from other prisoners on the cellblock that saved their butter pats and sugar packets. The pecans were smuggled in by other means. On my first full day of freedom I was compelled by my aunt, who is like a sister, to make a batch of candy at her house.

Later Laurie Lazer, a friend in San Francisco, helped me come up with the name Freelines. We liked the name because it sounds like pralines, which my candy is similar to, and I was finally free. It just made sense . . . Freelines.

Now that I AM FREE I hope to make life a little sweeter for you!

Try some of my Freelines, please visit my site or contact me at: www.KingsFreelines.com KingsFreelines@gmail.com

The Angola 3

Black Panthers and the Last Slave Plantation

$20.00 • ISBN: 978-1-60486-020-7

The Angola 3: Black Panthers and the Last Slave Plantation tells the gripping story of Robert King, Herman Wallace, and Albert Woodfox, men who have endured solitary confinement longer than any known living prisoner in the United States. Politicized through contact with the Black Panther Party while inside Louisiana's prisons, they formed one of the only prison Panther chapters in history and worked to organize other prisoners into a movement for the right to live like human beings. This feature length movie explores their extraordinary struggle for justice while incarcerated in Angola, a former slave plantation where institutionalized rape and murder made it known as one of the most brutal and racist prisons in the United States. The analysis of the Angola 3's political work, and the criminal cases used to isolate and silence them, occurs within the context of the widespread COINTELPRO being carried out in the 1960s and '70s by the FBI and state law enforcement against militant voices for change.

Narrated by Mumia Abu-Jamal, *The Angola 3* features interviews with former Panthers, political prisoners, and revolutionaries, including the Angola 3 themselves, and Bo Brown, Geronimo (ji Jaga) Pratt, Malik Rahim, Yuri Kochiyama, David Hilliard, Rod Coronado, Noelle Hanrahan, Kiilu Nyasha, Marion Brown, Luis Talamantez, Gail Shaw, and many others. Portions of the proceeds go to support the Angola 3. Features the music of Truth Universal written by Tajiri Kamau.

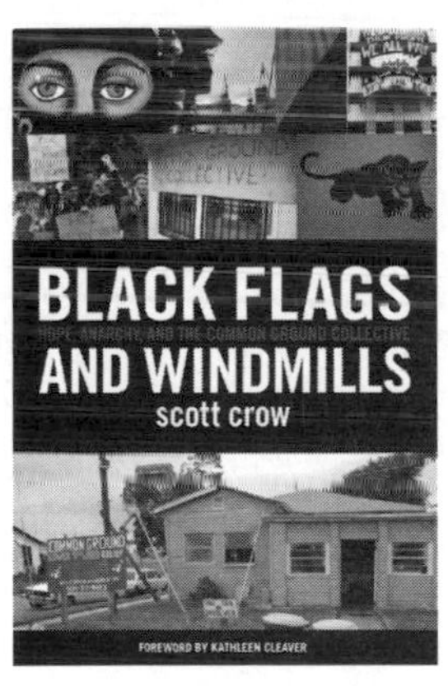

Black Flags and Windmills

Hope, Anarchy, and the Common Ground Collective

scott crow • Foreword by Kathleen Cleaver

$20.00 • ISBN: 978-1-60486-077-1

When both levees and governments failed in New Orleans in the Fall of 2005, scott crow headed into the political storm, cofounding a relief effort called the Common Ground Collective. In the absence of local government, FEMA, and the Red Cross, this unusual volunteer organization, based on "solidarity not charity," built medical clinics, set up food and water distribution, and created community gardens. They also resisted home demolitions, white militias, police brutality, and FEMA incompetence side by side with the people of New Orleans.

crow's vivid memoir maps the intertwining of his radical experience and ideas with Katrina's reality, and community efforts to translate ideals into action. It is a story of resisting indifference, rebuilding hope amidst collapse, and struggling against the grain. *Black Flags and Windmills* invites and challenges all of us to learn from our histories, and dream of better worlds. And gives us some of the tools to do so.

Resistance Behind Bars

The Struggles Of Incarcerated Women, 2nd Edition

Victoria Law • Introduction by Laura Whitehorn

$20.00 • ISBN: 978-1-60486-583-7

In 1974, women imprisoned at New York's maximum-security prison at Bedford Hills staged what is known as the August Rebellion. Protesting the brutal beating of a fellow prisoner, the women fought off guards, holding seven of them hostage, and took over sections of the prison.

While many have heard of the 1971 Attica prison uprising, the August Rebellion remains relatively unknown even in activist circles. *Resistance Behind Bars* is determined to challenge and change such oversights. As it examines daily struggles against appalling prison conditions and injustices, Resistance documents both collective organizing and individual resistance among women incarcerated in the U.S. Emphasizing women's agency in resisting the conditions of their confinement through forming peer education groups, clandestinely arranging ways for children to visit mothers in distant prisons and raising public awareness about their lives, *Resistance* seeks to spark further discussion and research into the lives of incarcerated women and galvanize much-needed outside support for their struggles.

This updated and revised edition of the 2009 PASS Award winning book includes a new chapter about transgender, transsexual, intersex, and gender-variant people in prison.

The Real Cost Of Prisons Comix

Edited by Lois Ahrens

Introduction by Craig Gilmore and Ruth Wilson Gilmore

$14.95 • ISBN: 978-1-60486-034-4

Winner of the 2008 PASS Award (Prevention for a Safer Society) from the National Council on Crime and Delinquency.

One out of every hundred adults in the U.S. is in prison. This book provides a crash course in what drives mass incarceration, the human and community costs, and how to stop the numbers from going even higher. This volume collects the three comic books published by the Real Cost of Prisons Project. The stories and statistical information in each comic book is thoroughly researched and documented.

Over 125,000 copies of the comic books have been printed and more than 100,000 have been sent to families of people who are incarcerated and to organizers and activists throughout the country. The book includes a chapter with descriptions about how the comix have been put to use in the work of organizers and activists in prison and in the "free world" by ESL teachers, high school teachers, college professors, students, and health care providers throughout the country. The demand for them is constant and the ways in which they are being used is inspiring.

Lucasville

The Untold Story of a Prison Uprising, 2nd ed.

Staughton Lynd • Preface by Mumia Abu-Jamal

$20.00 • ISBN: 978-1-60486-224-9

Lucasville tells the story of one of the longest prison uprisings in United States history. At the maximum security Southern Ohio Correctional Facility in Lucasville, Ohio, prisoners seized a major area of the prison on Easter Sunday, 1993. More than 400 prisoners held L block for eleven days. Nine prisoners alleged to have been informants, or "snitches," and one hostage correctional officer, were murdered. There was a negotiated surrender. Thereafter, almost wholly on the basis of testimony by prisoner informants who received deals in exchange, five spokespersons or leaders were tried and sentenced to death, and more than a dozen others received long sentences.

Lucasville examines both the causes of the disturbance, what happened during the eleven days, and the fairness of the trials. Particular emphasis is placed on the inter-racial character of the action, as evidenced in the slogans that were found painted on walls after the surrender: "Black and White Together," "Convict Unity," and "Convict Race."

Of the five men, three black and two white, who were sentenced to death, Mumia declares: "They rose above their status as prisoners, and became, for a few days in April 1993, what rebels in Attica had demanded a generation before them: men. As such, they did not betray each other; they did not dishonor each other; they reached beyond their prison "tribes" to reach commonality."

Let Freedom Ring

A Collection of Documents from the Movements to Free U.S. Political Prisoners

Editor Matt Meyer • Foreword by Adolfo Perez Esquivel • Afterwords by Ashanti Alston and Lynne Stewart

$37.95 • ISBN: 978-1-60486-035-1

Let Freedom Ring presents a two-decade sweep of essays, analyses, histories, interviews, resolutions, People's Tribunal verdicts, and poems by and about the scores of U.S. political prisoners and the campaigns to safeguard their rights and secure their freedom. In addition to an extensive section on the campaign to free death-row journalist Mumia Abu-Jamal, represented here are the radical movements that have most challenged the U.S. empire from within: Black Panthers and other Black liberation fighters, Puerto Rican independentistas, Indigenous sovereignty activists, white anti-imperialists, environmental and animal rights militants, Arab and Muslim activists, Iraq war resisters, and others. Contributors in and out of prison detail the repressive methods—from long-term isolation to sensory deprivation to politically inspired parole denial—used to attack these freedom fighters, some still caged after 30+ years. This invaluable resource guide offers inspiring stories of the creative, and sometimes winning, strategies to bring them home.

Love and Struggle

My Life in SDS, the Weather Underground, and Beyond

David Gilbert • Foreword by Boots Riley

$22.00 • ISBN: 978-1-60486-319-2

A nice Jewish boy from suburban Boston—hell, an Eagle Scout!—David Gilbert arrived at Columbia University just in time for the explosive Sixties. From the early anti-Vietnam War protests to the founding of SDS, from the Columbia Strike to the tragedy of the Townhouse, Gilbert was on the scene: as organizer, theoretician, and above all, activist. He was among the first militants who went underground to build the clandestine resistance to war and racism known as "Weatherman." And he was among the last to emerge, in captivity, after the disaster of the 1981 Brink's robbery, an attempted expropriation that resulted in four deaths and long prison terms. In this extraordinary memoir, written from the maximum-security prison where he has lived for almost thirty years, Gilbert tells the intensely personal story of his own Long March from liberal to radical to revolutionary.

Today a beloved and admired mentor to a new generation of activists, he assesses with rare humor, with an understanding stripped of illusions, and with uncommon candor the errors and advances, terrors and triumphs of the Sixties and beyond. It's a battle that was far from won, but is still not lost: the struggle to build a new world, and the love that drives that effort. A cautionary tale and a how-to as well, Love and Struggle is a book as candid, as uncompromising, and as humane as its author.

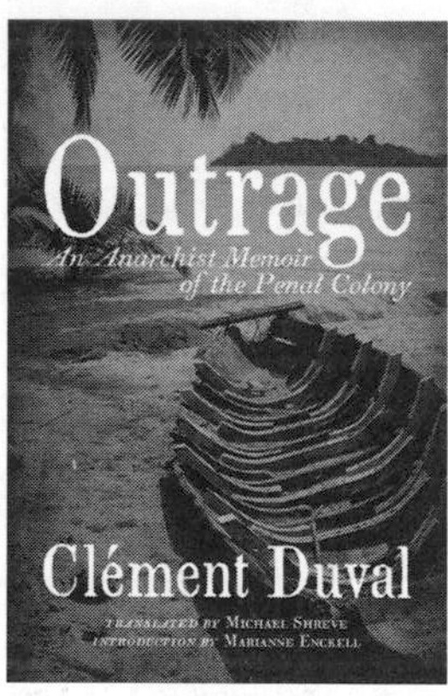

Outrage

An Anarchist Memoir of the Penal Colony

Clément Duval • Translated by Michael Shreve • Introduction by Marianne Enckell

$20.00 • ISBN: 978-1-60486-500-4

In 1887, Clément Duval joined the tens of thousands of convicts sent to the "dry guillotine" of the French penal colonies. Few survived and fewer were able to tell the stories of their life in that hell. Duval spent fourteen years doing hard labor—espousing the values of anarchism and demonstrating the ideals by being a living example the entire time—before making his daring escape and arriving in New York City, welcomed by the Italian and French anarchists there.

This is much more than an historical document about the anarchist movement and the penal colony. It is a remarkable story of survival by one man's self-determination, energy, courage, loyalty, and hope. It was thanks to being true and faithful to his ideals that Duval survived life in this hell. Unlike the well-known prisoner Papillon, who arrived and dramatically escaped soon after Duval, he encouraged his fellow prisoners to practice mutual aid, through their deeds and not just their words. It is a call to action for mindful, conscious people to fight for their rights to the very end, to never give up or give in.

More than just a story of a life or a testament of ideals, here is a monument to the human spirit and a war cry for freedom and justice.